Everyone should be aware ... n
self-awareness. She has a ... s
complex and dynamic subje ... ·r
compromising on the rigorous academic basis for her insights. This book unlocks decades of learning and experience – first in the Royal Navy; then as a professional leadership coach; subsequently as a trainer of the next generation of coaches; and ultimately as a leading academic researcher at Henley Business School. In these pages, she brilliantly makes the case and provides the tools for us all to make the journey towards reaching our true potential both as leaders and as coaches by understanding the art and science of becoming more self-aware.

Darren Henley CBE,
CEO, Arts Council England

You Are Not As Self-Aware As You Think You Are is a beautifully written book that takes a deeply personal and immersive dive into the importance of self-awareness for leaders. The book is full of useful tools and techniques for self-reflection and personal growth. Having experienced first-hand Dr Carden's skill as an executive coach, I would thoroughly recommend this book for any leader wishing to enhance their effectiveness as a leader.

Matt Cook,
Chief Fire Officer/Chief Executive of Avon Fire and Rescue Service

Anyone Julia has coached will recognize how much practical wisdom and useful structure she has captured in this book. Beyond this, she has created a thought-provoking book that also works at a deeper level. Julia challenges conventional notions of self-awareness by raising incisive questions about the interplay between the inner self and our connections with others.

The open style, enriched by evocative quotes, ignites inquiry into the systemic, multi-dimensional nature of personality. It is a transformative read for anyone seeking to lead authentically and seamlessly harness genuine inter- and intra-personal integration.

Dr Chris Dalton,
Associate Professor of Management Learning,
Henley Business School

This book was an excellent read and has helped me realize that I wasn't as self-aware as I had initially believed. By reading it, I developed a much deeper understanding of the concept and acknowledged the effort and dedication needed to cultivate it. Although the process may be demanding, I am fully committed to the journey, as the book compellingly emphasized why self-awareness is a fundamental aspect of effective leadership—whether for those currently leading or aspiring to lead.

Scott Stephens,
CEO, FORTH® Group of Companies

Clearly being self-aware makes a person a more effective leader or manager. But what does this mean in practice? In this thoroughly enjoyable and well-researched book, Carden sets this all out by taking the subject apart and then methodically reconstructing it, setting out the forms of self-awareness, with some gripping examples. The book challenges how a leader can be effective leading others before they even can understand themselves, which is so valid and explored at length. It talks about the advantages of being curious and asking questions, how to adopt a growth mindset and guard against thinking you know it all. You should be comfortable with not knowing everything in a world where the 'doing of the work is the win, rather than the work or the outcome'. Understanding this sets you on the path towards self-awareness and away from self-delusion or hubris.

In the book Carden cleverly takes you on a voyage of self-discovery and makes the reader stop and think about their own personal experience. This is genuinely a book which can change your perceptions on life and even includes some small advice about taking some time out if the revelations become too challenging. It is painstakingly researched and full of strong references and quotes which enhance its authority and standing.

I would highly recommend this book to anyone and certainly anyone keen to enhance their management style. I found it utterly gripping and insightful and one of those books which make you really stop and think about yourself. While it has the flavour of an academic treatise, Carden writes in a clear and compelling style which makes it highly readable and gripping and so it is well suited to anyone interested in becoming better at what they do. It is certainly a must-read manual for coaches – but is more than this too, and good for any leader or manager keen to enhance their ability. I was completely engrossed from page one.

Alistair Halliday,
CEO, Forces Employment Charity

This thoughtful and genuinely useful book on self-awareness is full of real-life examples, practical tips and occasional personal insights. In particular, Julia uses different highly relatable metaphors throughout the book to help the reader to really grasp the seemingly intangible threads of self-awareness. My favourite had to be the 'ingredients' metaphor – it captures the layered, evolving nature of what it means to really know ourselves and how we relate to others. This style, together with some really inspiring quotes which themselves caused me to stop and reflect, meant that this is a great resource for prompting reflection and thinking as the book unfolds. Using an easy and relaxed writing style, Julia offers a clear, grounded approach that makes the complex feel manageable, without oversimplifying. What I appreciated most was the flexibility and fluidity of the book. Each section invites you to start where it feels right, giving you something meaningful to reflect on with signposts to different parts of the book depending on your own interest. Whether you're a leader, a coach, or simply curious about your own development, this book is a valuable and insightful companion.

Clancy Murphy,
Coach and Business Consultant

This book is a tool for self-discovery. The reflective questions prompt you to pause and consider self at a deeper level, with knowledge and awareness building section upon section, chapter upon chapter. Dr Carden effectively blends the evidence on the topic of self-awareness with examples from her own practice and vulnerable reflections on her own journey towards building self-awareness, in this practical, easy-to-read text.

Professor Rebecca Jones,
Professor in Coaching and Behavioural Change,
Henley Business School

Julia's extensive coaching and leadership experience informs a highly practical and actionable set of insights on self-awareness. A 'must-read' and a 'must-do' for leaders at every level, it challenges traditional notions and unexamined beliefs about self-awareness and how it informs and shapes how leaders behave and perform.

Rob Lewis,
Founding Director, Mission Performance

I thought I was fairly self-aware, and then I read this book. In an easy to engage with style Julia invited me to face the reality that I probably wasn't! Then helped me take those steps to not just understand the subject, but she helped me delve into who I am and how I show up to others. Uncomfortable at times, but strangely addictive, I find myself coming back to this book again and again. Each time getting something new and insightful.

If you are a leader or work in coaching or any form of human development this book is for you. If like I did, you think you have got this self-awareness cracked, then put this book at the top of your reading list. Your team and clients will thank you, and you will notice the difference.

Jim Macleod CB CVO,
Executive Coach and Leadership Consultant

What supports great leadership? What carries leaders through challenge and change? It is the universal skill of self-awareness. Dr Julia Carden invites us to reconsider self-awareness not as a fixed trait we either have or do not, but as a living, relational process shaped by both our inner world and how others perceive us.

Carden challenges the traditional, individualistic notion of self-awareness and instead highlights its deeply relational and embodied nature. It is not just cognitive. It lives in our emotions, our sensations, the subtle shifts of breath and posture, the ways we respond to others and the ways they, in turn, shape our awareness of ourselves. Self-awareness, she argues, is not something we achieve in isolation but something that unfolds dynamically through movement, feedback and interaction.

Through deep research, compelling case studies and thoughtful inquiry, Carden unpacks the complexity of self-awareness, showing that it is a fluid and ever-evolving skill, rather than a static quality to master. She invites us beyond self-reflection and into a more relational and responsive way of knowing ourselves; one that requires curiosity, openness and a willingness to receive feedback that may disrupt our sense of self.

For leaders, this book offers a fresh reframe. It moves us away from the illusion of certainty and into the reality of presence, responsiveness and relational intelligence. It calls us to question how we construct our own awareness, how we co-create it with others and how this, in turn, shapes the way we lead, enable and connect.

If you believe that transformation happens not just in the mind but in the body, in relationships and in the spaces in between, then this offers a fresh perspective. Carden reminds us that self-awareness, particularly in leadership, is not a destination but a practice: one that invites us to keep listening, noticing and evolving.

Dr Eunice Aquilina,
Founder of eaconsult and author of Embodying Authenticity (2016) and Stepping into Your Power (2021)

I'm not someone who reads many self-development books but much like Julia's coaching style, this book is both practical and accessible, so useful for the person who wants to develop their self-awareness but is unsure whether they are on the right path.

Full of helpful references, reflective questions and explanations, there's a lifetime of thinking and work here. This book is for someone open to self-development. It fills me with hope and excitement for my future.

Enwezor Nzegwu,
Enterprise Architect and Coachee

Having had the chance to read Julia Carden's *You're Not As Self-Aware As You Think You Are* in draft form, I can say it's an incredibly useful book – not just for leaders, but for anyone coaching or consulting with them. Reading it, I reflected on how valuable it would have been when I was in leadership roles myself, and how it now sharpens my practice as an executive and team coach. It's a book that prompts deep reflection, not just for the people we coach, but for ourselves too. If we're helping others build self-awareness, we should be doing the same work. A must-read for leaders and coaches alike.

Dirk Anthony MSc PCC,
Executive Coach and Consultant

It's very easy to go through a career believing one is self-aware and feeling open and accepting of feedback. Now that I have really invested time, with the help of the book, I truly understand what self-awareness is, how to develop it and why I need to put more effort into developing it. This is an invaluable book to any leader or manager who is serious about performing at their best. The wealth of research is supported by a plethora of references, and it is packed full of thought-provoking questions and useful exercises to help any reader begin (or continue) on their journey of truly becoming self-aware. This is an invaluable book to any leader or manager who is serious about performing at their best.

Myles Dawson,
Entrepreneur and Business Founder

If you're an executive coach and like me you already thought you were fully self-aware or had self-awareness figured out – think again. Julia Carden's *You Are Not as Self-Aware as You Think You Are* is the kind of book that stops you mid-sentence and makes you rethink your perceptions, constructs and the questions you're asking yourself. It's smart, educational and as you would expect from any of Julia's sessions, thought provoking enough to last for days. Be prepared to be challenged, think deeper and you will get comfortable with the fact that you'll never be as 'self-aware as you think you are'.

Brian Mapley,
VP of Sales UK, Adyen & Executive Coach

A must-read for every leader navigating uncertainty. As someone who leads a large team, I found this book not only helpful and supportive, but also deeply thought-provoking. It challenged me to reflect on my own self-awareness and re-examine my role as a leader in today's fast-changing world.

Julia brings a new level of clarity to what leadership truly means and how we can all grow as individuals and find more in ourselves than we know is there. More importantly, it underscored just how critical this work is in a dynamic business environment.

I'm now even more convinced that developing our self-awareness isn't optional – it's essential for leading effectively through uncertainty. I highly recommend this book to anyone in a leadership position. It's not just insightful – it's transformative.

Jon Fryer,
Franchise Director, Sytner Group

Why true **self-awareness** is at the core of great leadership

You Are Not As Self-Aware As You Think You Are

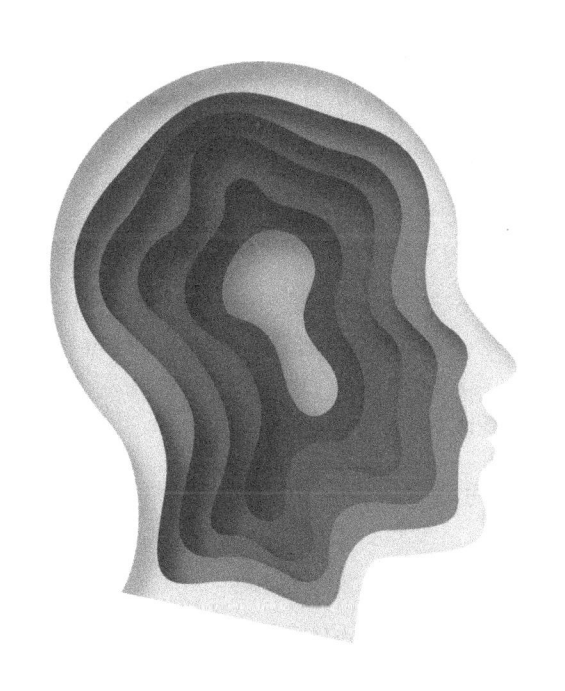

DR JULIA CARDEN

PhD MSc PCC FCIPD

First published in Great Britain by Practical Inspiration Publishing, 2025

© Julia Carden, 2025

The moral rights of the author have been asserted.

ISBN   9781788608022 (paperback)
       9781788608015 (hardback)
       9781788608039 (ebook)

All rights reserved. This book, or any portion thereof, may not be reproduced without the express written permission of the publisher.

Every effort has been made to trace copyright holders and to obtain their permission for the use of copyright material. The publisher apologizes for any errors or omissions and would be grateful if notified of any corrections that should be incorporated in future reprints or editions of this book.

EU GPSR representative: LOGOS EUROPE, 9 rue Nicolas Poussin, LA ROCHELLE 17000, France Contact@logoseurope.eu

Want to bulk-buy copies of this book for your team and colleagues? We can customize the content and co-brand *You Are Not As Self-Aware As You Think You Are* to suit your business's needs.

Please email info@practicalinspiration.com for more details.

Practical Inspiration Publishing

MIX
Paper | Supporting responsible forestry
FSC® C013604
www.fsc.org

Acknowledgements

Whilst the contents of this book stem from my PhD research, its origins are in my own leadership journey and subsequent development as an executive coach. Along that journey I have learnt and gathered wisdom from a wide variety of teachers, peers, coaches, mentors and clients, as well as all those who contributed to my research. My learning and the perspectives I have gained along the way have been intertwined with my PhD data and results to bring this book alive. I therefore wish to thank all of those who have contributed to my ongoing journey for getting me to the point where I feel 'good enough' to write this book.

Thanks must go to my family, my husband Peter and son, Freddie, who are fed up with me talking about self-awareness! Also, I wish to acknowledge my PhD supervisors, Professors Rebecca Jones and Jonathan Passmore, who helped me throughout my research, guiding me and challenging my thinking.

I also want to extend my thanks to all those who have helped me develop my own self-awareness. There are many inspiring trainers, educators, colleagues and friends who have supported me in this aspect, but special thanks go to Professor Alison Hardingham; Mick Stott for all the NLP training; my coaches Linda Aspey and Tony Melville; my coaching supervisors Tracy Barr, Eunice Aquilina and Jo Birch; my Thinking Partner Javier Fernandez; and my therapist Stephen Burt.

Contents

Acknowledgements		xi
Foreword by Vice Admiral Sir Martin Connell KCB CBE		xvii
Introduction		1
Part 1:	Thinking about self-awareness and the starting point	7
Chapter 1:	Why are we talking about self-awareness?	9
Chapter 2:	So, you think you know what self-awareness is	23
Chapter 3:	Doing the work: where to start?	31
Part 2:	Self-awareness: introducing the inter-personal components	47
Chapter 4:	Developing self-awareness: the inter-personal component of others' perceptions	53
Chapter 5:	Developing self-awareness: the inter-personal component of behaviours	63

Part 3:	Self-awareness: introducing the intra-personal components	71
Chapter 6:	Developing self-awareness: the intra-personal component of values and beliefs	75
Chapter 7:	Developing self-awareness: the intra-personal component of strengths and weaknesses	97
Chapter 8:	Developing self-awareness: the intra-personal component of motivations	109
Chapter 9:	Developing self-awareness: the intra-personal component of internal mental state	119
Chapter 10:	Developing self-awareness: the intra-personal component of physiological responses	129
Part 4:	Self-connection the route to leading through uncertainty: an introduction	137
Chapter 11: Self-connection for great leadership		139
Chapter 12: Self-awareness or self-delusion		157
Chapter 13: Facilitating self-awareness in others		165
Chapter 14: Final words		175
Appendix: Other helpful resources		179
References		181
Index		185

Figures and tables

Figure 1 Relationship between self-awareness
         and leadership skills   15

Figure 2 The components of self-awareness   25

Figure 3 The jigsaw of self-awareness development   36

Figure 4 Logical levels of self-awareness   77

Figure 5 From self-awareness to self-connection
         and leading others   141

Table 1 Self-deception and self-delusion   160

Foreword

Throughout my 38-year career in the Royal Navy and Defence, I have become increasingly focused on my own self-awareness and abilities as a leader, particularly in the more senior positions I have taken on. Many senior executives quickly discover, perhaps for some too late, that what got us to where we are now – specialized expertise, skills and competencies – will simply not suffice for where we need to be. With a broadened range of responsibility comes an imperative for increased empathy, humility and much better communication skills. You come to accept that complex problems rarely have simple solutions, and that you need to be comfortable dealing with uncertainty, and with being able to ask open questions, actively seeking and listening to alternative viewpoints, and delegating to others the things you may have previously enjoyed doing yourself.

While I now routinely engage and embrace executive coaching and 360-degree reporting, and have excellent reverse mentors, I'm surprised that this has only really been a factor for the latter part of my career and I wish it had been in place much earlier on. But there is plenty we can all do to equip ourselves as leaders and I therefore consider self-awareness to be a quality of critical importance to any serious modern, senior leader.

Before reading this book I, like many of my colleagues and other senior leaders, perceived that I was sufficiently self-aware and I therefore found the title of this book somewhat curious, perhaps even challenging. Self-awareness is such a widely used term, I was convinced I knew what it was; however, this book has been illuminating, and I now realize that I am perhaps not as self-aware as I initially thought. I now understand the complex nature of the construct and recognize the effort and commitment required to develop and nurture it. The book also shines a light on the importance of self-awareness to develop the self-connection required to lead in this increasingly uncertain and volatile world we all live in. Having read through the book I am firmly persuaded that self-awareness should be considered as a key competency during selection processes and be a part of all leadership training.

Julia's book is not simply another self-help manual promising quick fixes and superficial insights. Rather, it is a rigorously researched and deeply insightful exploration of the chasm that often exists between our *perceived* self and our *actual* self. We assume we know ourselves, that our intentions are clear, and our actions are perceived as we intend. Yet, as the book so compellingly demonstrates, this is rarely the case. We are riddled with blind spots, cognitive biases and ingrained patterns of behaviour that distort our self-image and undermine our effectiveness, and we often assume we're communicating our intent with clarity and purpose when in fact the opposite may be true. In the high-stakes environment of senior leadership, particularly when matters of national security are at stake, these blind spots can have catastrophic consequences.

While I reluctantly accept that, as a busy leader with limited periods of free time, I don't get to read as much as I would wish, I did find this book easily accessible and digestible. Whilst it is based on Julia's doctoral research, it is practical and relatable, with clear signposting so that you can dip in and out as time allows. There are several exercises and lots of case studies bringing the content to life.

Being grounded in empirical research combined with personal and practical experience Julia's approach is refreshing. Her vulnerability in sharing her personal stories as well as case studies brings humility to the underlying expertise and knowledge. This book possesses a rare combination of intellectual rigor and practical wisdom, making her work both academically sound and immediately applicable. Moreover, Julia's approach is marked by a deep empathy and a genuine desire to support others to realize their full potential. She understands that the journey to self-awareness is not always easy, and she provides the reader with the tools and support they need to navigate the challenges along the way.

You Are Not As Self-Aware As You Think You Are is not just a book; it is a call to action. It is a challenge to confront our own blind spots and to embark on a journey of self-discovery. In this digital age increasingly defined by complexity, chaos and uncertainty, the ability to understand ourselves and our impact on others is more important than ever.

I commend Julia for her work and encourage every reader to embrace the insights contained within these pages. By cultivating greater self-awareness and developing deeper self-connection we can bring greater humanity to our roles in support of transformational leadership.

Vice Admiral Sir Martin Connell KCB CBE
Second Sea Lord
London April 2025

Introduction

> *'To know thyself'*
> *(Temple of Apollo Maxim, at Delphi)*

I was recently talking to a senior leader, and I was discussing with him who and what he used to support him in the lonely position of senior leadership. His response to me was 'I don't think I need anyone; I am very self-aware.' In that moment, with that claim, I knew he wasn't. I was not surprised that he said this as I have heard several leaders either make similar statements or send team members to be coached to improve their self-awareness believing that, as the leader, they are *'all sorted'*. Therefore, I did not respond to this comment and was quietly amused. After all, before my research, I too thought that I was self-aware and had been developing my self-awareness for several years – how wrong I was!

What is the book about and why is it important?

The reality is that most of us don't really know what self-awareness is, and therefore how can we be self-aware? Is it even important? Yes, because when you are self-aware and know thyself, you can be the authentic leader you want to be. After all, who you are, is how you lead. I remember asking one leader, who had just started a new job 'who are you as a leader?' He was floored and struggled to answer the question – I am sure if I had asked his team, they would have had a view on this, but who he wanted and believed himself to be and who his team thought he was, would likely be incongruent. This lack of awareness can lead to challenges and tensions in leading a team, with the prospect of the leader lacking confidence, being unpredictable and probably experiencing internal struggles and tensions. Through working on his self-awareness the leader was able to get a clearer sense of who he was as a leader, so he then showed up feeling grounded and centred, was more confident and projected greater clarity. This resulted in a team that experienced less internal conflict, was more cohesive, and was able to tackle challenges with confidence and a clear sense of direction. A self-aware leader should be able to answer the question 'if I was to get your team in here, what would they say about you?' And, in addition to answering the question, they would have a sense of inner calm, understanding and contentment with their reply.

This level of inner peace and contentment projected by the self-confident leader is what I would describe as a self-connected leader, they truly know themselves. In working with these leaders, I have observed they have been able to overcome leadership challenges, be those project/business or individual/people ones, despite an understanding that they won't have all the answers or be perfect in their chosen way ahead. This means that they can seek support when appropriate and explore other perspectives and ideas without their ego or self-esteem being undermined. This self-connectedness is achieved through getting clear on their values and checking whether their behaviours are in line with those values – all through the lens of self-awareness.

Part of this self-connection is about self-acceptance, a knowing, belief and embodiment that you are good enough. Self-acceptance is about accepting all aspects of ourselves, including what I call our 'uglies' (i.e. our shadow side, weaknesses, past mistakes and history). This enables us to be at our best without what Brene Brown calls 'hustling for worthiness' (Brown, 2022). I encounter many leaders who state and claim they have 'imposter syndrome' which can lead to them seeking validation and affirmation. Working on beliefs and ensuring limiting, unhelpful beliefs are minimized, and helpful beliefs are maximized through self-awareness work will support them in overcoming this and accepting who they are (self-acceptance).

I am also increasingly seeing overwhelmed leaders who are stressed and over-loaded and who have ended up dedicating their lives to their work, often mistaking their work for their life – using the concept of Naomi Shragai (2021) who wrote a book titled *The Man who Mistook his Job for his Life*. This is the new norm, because we are now available 24/7, 365 days of the year wherever we are, and there are multiple ways of being contacted, being available and being 'on duty'. Learning how to lead and find time in this new norm, and then actually thriving, stems from the self-connection which is developed through self-awareness. This work can help identify what is most important to you.

Other clients come to me wanting to develop the capacity to handle uncertainty and sit with not knowing. I liken this to the poet Keats' concept of negative capability, which he describes as 'capable of being in uncertainties, mysteries and doubts, without any irritable reaching after fact and reason'. This is about leading in the current volatile world you are faced with, also known as VUCA (Volatile, Uncertain, Complex and Ambiguous). Once you have developed self-connection, found inner peace and settled your ego, you will find that you can lead more effectively in this space and be better at facing uncertainty.

In summary, self-awareness is vital as it will make you a better leader – you will have inner peace and clarity on who you are as a leader, be confident and grounded, be able to overcome imposter syndrome, and you will be more effective at tackling leadership challenges and the uncertainty that arises in the modern world.

In supporting you on the journey to self-awareness, this book will explore what self-awareness is, how it leads to self-connection and why that is important, the links between self-awareness and leadership skills, how to develop self-awareness and how to avoid self-delusion. You will see that the book is divided into four parts. Part 1 focuses on the 'what' and 'why' of self-awareness. Parts 2 and 3 deep-dive into each of the components of self-awareness, explaining what they are and how to develop each. Part 4 leads on to self-connection, the exploration of when self-awareness tips into self-delusion, self-deception or hubris, and how, as leaders, you can facilitate the development of self-awareness in others.

Socrates identified that self-reflection through thought-provoking questions is an effective approach to 'knowing self', so with that in mind there are questions and exercises throughout the book to reflect on in service of you developing and deepening your self-awareness as you read. You will have responses as you read, and the book content will likely trigger a reaction in you; notice these responses and reactions and be curious as to what they might be revealing about you. You might wish to capture what is emerging for you as you read, or you can download the questions and exercises as individual handouts from the website which accompanies this book at **www.youarenotasselfawareasyouthink.com**. There are also supporting resources from other writers and thinkers at the end of each chapter and in the appendix at the end.

Who is this book for?

This book is primarily written for leaders who wish to expand their self-awareness and increase their leadership effectiveness in today's volatile world. It is also for executive coaches who wish to deepen their practice and learn to sit with uncertainty and not knowing. By the end of this book, readers will gain a better understanding of themselves, develop practical strategies for enhancing their self-awareness, and learn how to navigate complexity with greater confidence.

The stories and examples in this book are based on many years of experience and the multitude of leaders and clients I have worked with – although I have changed details so they are not attached to one individual. If you recognize yourself in these stories that will be by chance.

So why have I written this book?

Since I began my leadership journey I have been interested in self-awareness, and on a quest to become self-aware. The 'unknown to self, and unknown to others' box of Johari's Window had a tantalizing allure of 'you need to delve here to really find the secret to self.' I think I was under some false illusion that once I got to a fully self-aware state, I would in some way be a complete, whole and authentic leader and coach. I now know that I will never be done, but that my developmental work is supporting me in finding inner peace and contentment. It was when I started my Masters in Coaching and Behavioural Change that I realized the importance of self-awareness in terms of its impact on how I was showing up in my practice, and later how self-awareness supports the capability and capacity to sit with uncertainty. This is what is transformational in how we show up as leaders, because who we are is how we lead and there is an increasing need to lead through uncertainty.

My interest and passion in this topic led to me undertaking a PhD to research this further and that research, along with my lifelong journey in this space, is what underpins this book.

As an aside

The book cover design is symbolic of my own history. My leadership journey started as a WRNS (Women's Royal Naval Service) Officer with training at HMS RALEIGH and BRNC DARTMOUTH. As a WRNS officer I wore blue rank stripes. During my service the WRNS were fully integrated into the Royal Navy and we lost our blue stripes and changed to gold stripes – hence the Navy and Gold colours. Symbols are an important part of what makes us who we are, and this is symbolic for me. I am therefore privileged to have the foreword written by the Second Sea Lord, Vice Admiral Sir Martin Connell.

Moving on

I invite you, as Brene Brown (2015) says, to be open to uncertainty, get curious and step into your vulnerability, and be brave. By becoming self-aware change will start.

> ### For Reflection
>
> Before you leap out of the starting gate pause and ask yourself:
>
> - What do I believe self-awareness is?
> - Why is self-awareness important to me?
> - How self-aware do I believe I am? (scale 1–10, with 10 being extremely self-aware)

PART 1
THINKING ABOUT SELF-AWARENESS AND THE STARTING POINT

> *'The moment we become aware of something,*
> *we become accountable for it.'*
> Anon

When I was doing my research I asked others, 'how would you define self-awareness?' Those answering struggled to give a clear definition and struggled to name individual elements of what it is. Most of us believe we know what it is because it is such a popular and widely talked about concept. So, it is no surprise that most of us who have heard of the term believe that we know what it is and have developed it. I have also heard leaders talking about self-knowledge and self-consciousness as if they are the same as self-awareness, and sometimes as something different. This is all very confusing and unless you have clarity on what self-awareness is you are unlikely to develop it or understand how it is benefitting you as a leader.

Therefore, this initial part of the book will introduce you to what self-awareness is and why you should be putting effort into developing it.

I also hope that these early chapters will challenge your perception that you think you are self-aware, because if you don't really know what self-awareness is – how can you be? This was the case for the leader mentioned in the introduction and is the reality for most of us.

Doing this work will enhance your leadership effectiveness, and support you in today's world, so I invite you to jump in, start the work and, above all, enjoy the discovery.

Chapter 1
Why are we talking about self-awareness?

> *'To know thyself is the beginning of wisdom.'*
> Socrates, c.469–c.399 BC

Throughout the time of running my own business, I have been asked to design Assessment and Development Centres to assess self-awareness, coach leaders and managers to develop it, and use psychometric personality profiles to build awareness in both individuals and teams. I, like many coaches, consultants and leaders had mistakenly been thinking I was doing just that, i.e. assessing or developing self-awareness. I now know that there was no way I could have been doing this with any certainty. The primary reason for this being that rarely is self-awareness defined with any granularity. Indeed, it is often confused with other terms about self, e.g. self-knowledge and self-consciousness. This is why I say, 'we are not as self-aware as we think we are', because how can we be self-aware if we don't know what self-awareness is?

> **For Reflection**
>
> ▸ What do you think it is?
> ▸ How do you know you have developed or been developing it?

It is not a surprise that self-awareness is talked about with confidence, as the term has been around for centuries, with its root in the ancient Greek philosophy of Socrates. Socrates alluded to the importance of self-awareness with his perspective that knowing yourself, by being aware of personal performance limits and having an understanding of strengths and weaknesses, was a route through to wisdom and success.

Even knowing what it is does not mean we are self-aware, because it is an ever evolving, multi-layered, complex and dynamic construct and we are never the finished product. This is because every time we work alongside others and tackle new challenges, we learn something more about self. As Pema Chodron says, 'we work on ourselves in order to work with others; we work with others in order to work on ourselves' (Chodron, 2008; p. 78). Chapter 2 will describe what self-awareness is in detail, and if you are already bought into why it is important, you might wish to skip straight to the next Chapter.

> **For Reflection**
>
> Thinking about Pema Chodron's quote, here are an initial couple of questions you might ask yourself:
>
> ▸ As a leader what's the work I need to do on self to be at my best?

> What am I learning about myself from working with my team and those around me?

Coming back to the leader I mentioned in the introduction, my initial question of 'who or what do you do to support you?' must have prompted some reflection because he later asked me to draw up a proposal of what I thought he needed to work on and how he might tackle it. We've not yet done the work. This is important because to develop self-awareness you must be motivated and ready to engage. I didn't think he was ready, yet it was interesting that he was sending his team members to me to develop their self-awareness and enhance their leadership skills. My sense was that the team did not hold him in high esteem; I suspect he had other views. To lead requires personal insight and that only comes from being curious about oneself.

Why is self-awareness important to your leadership?

If you are a busy leader who has already done lots of leadership development, you may be asking 'why bother?' Self-awareness is a key differentiator between mediocre and fabulous leaders, and this concept has already been widely discussed by writers such as Jim Collins (2001) in his book *Good to Great*. Who we are is how we lead, and how we show up in all aspects of our lives. Therefore, getting to grips with what shapes and informs our behaviours, responses and relationships is hugely beneficial, because how can we understand others if we don't first understand ourselves? The leaders I have worked with who have spent time getting curious about 'why they behave in the way they do' tend to ask better questions in conversations with team members and this enhances team engagement and commitment.

Going back to the Socratic origins

- ▶ Socrates believed a life without self-reflection and the exploration of understanding self was a life not worth living.

- ▶ He also identified that self-awareness was the premise and foundation for living ethically and morally, something that is required to embrace difference in the workplace today.

- ▶ In essence, he perceived that self-awareness was not just an intellectual exercise, but a moral imperative.

This was because he argued that by diligently examining ourselves and seeking truth, we can live a more fulfilling and virtuous life. This is aligned to the inner peace and contentment I talked about in the introduction. Nevertheless, it is impractical and unrealistic to have the expectation to be experiencing this 100% of the time. The aim though is to be as close to the 100% as possible, and the more self-work we do the closer we will get. It is tough to reach this level of focus when there are so many competing priorities on our time, and when the world around us can trigger us into 'survival' instinct. However, gaining awareness can start the change – without this awareness we can't change. When working with leaders and managers, initiating self-awareness can have huge benefits in terms of them enhancing their leadership effectiveness.

> **Case Study**
>
> I worked with a very senior leader who had lost a sense of perspective on his life and was finding he 'never switched off' – perhaps unsurprisingly his health suffered. By working through his values and beliefs, his thought processes and the behaviours he wished others to see, over time he was able to start taking some small steps for change and began applying a few simple and attainable principles to his week to guide his choices. This resulted in better sleep and him becoming a more productive leader. Achieving this sort of balance is often down to getting clear on boundaries and also being able to say 'no'. The inability to set boundaries and say 'no' is often down to misguided and limiting beliefs.

Self-awareness is also the starting point for self-connection which in turn leads to greater and more effective connection with others (this is discussed further in Chapter 11). This is critical in the creation of high-performance teams and is an enabler for leading in the VUCA (Volatile, Uncertain, Complex and Ambiguous) world that we all lead, live and work in.

Self-awareness in relation to leadership skills

The work on self-awareness comes alongside or after understanding and developing basic leadership skills and knowledge. It always amazes me when organizations promote people to leadership roles on the premise that they are good at their job but give them no training on how to lead, in terms of leadership principles, models and frameworks.

> **Case Study**
>
> I recently had a request from a team leader to coach a junior leader around leadership skills with the aim to improve the latter's confidence. Training in the fundamentals of leadership may well induce confidence through an understanding of the principles. Whilst I know the leader is working with genuine positive intent to help his team member, the priority is around the development of basic leadership skills rather than coaching. However, coaching might support this young leader if the lack of confidence is stemming from personal beliefs and thinking traps. Nevertheless, my experience tells me that I may well be coaching the team leader around his self-awareness to gain clarity, so as to best determine the way ahead for this team member. The self-awareness dynamic is often akin to a dipole working in two directions.

Although I am focusing on self-awareness in this book, I want to emphasize the importance of also having some training and development around leadership skills and the 'how to' lead. This is one thing the military does particularly well in terms of leadership training. The link between the two is shown in the simple four-box model in Figure 1.

This framework draws on the thinking of Goffee and Jones (Goffee and Jones, 2006), Blakey and Day (2012) and my own research (Carden, Passmore and Jones, 2022a). By leadership skills on the x-axis, I am referring to the skills and tools likely to be taught and developed on leadership development programmes. What I perceive as the 'doing' of the work. Self-awareness is defined in Chapter 2.

Why are we talking about self-awareness? | 15

```
  ^
  |
  |   ┌─────────────┐           ┌─────────────┐
  |   │ Leading with│           │Leading with │
  |   │empathy; the │           │  wisdom;    │
S |   │  over-      │           │ authentic   │
e |   │whelmed      │           │  leader     │
l |   │  leader     │           │             │
f |   └─────────────┘           └─────────────┘
- |
A |─────────────────────────────────────────────
w |
a |   ┌─────────────┐           ┌─────────────┐
r |   │             │           │ Focused on  │
e |   │The unaware  │           │ outcomes    │
n |   │and clumsy   │           │and results; │
e |   │  leader     │           │ needs to be │
s |   │             │           │the central  │
s |   │             │           │   focus     │
  |   └─────────────┘           └─────────────┘
  |
  |─────────────────────────────────────────────>
              ┌──────────────────┐
              │ Leadership Skills│
              └──────────────────┘
```

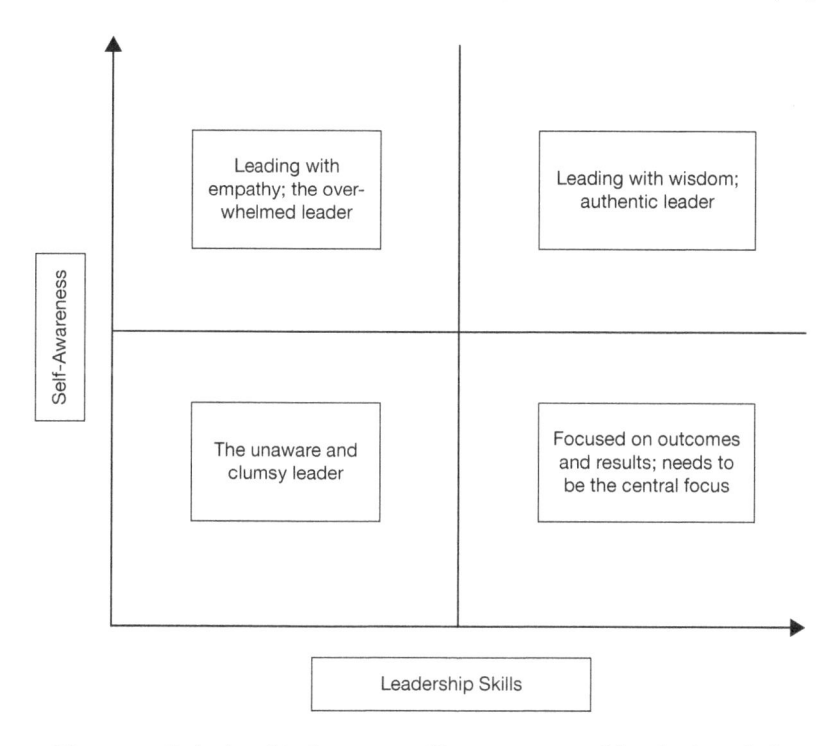

Figure 1: Relationship between self-awareness and leadership skills

With high self-awareness and low leadership skills (the top left quadrant), the leader is likely to be leading with empathy and humanity. They will have built strong relationships with their team and are likely to be well liked. However, they will probably be overwhelmed by not knowing how to have effective performance management conversations and due to ineffective delegation. Performance management discussions are likely to be tough as will be giving feedback (all the skills learnt through leadership development). Due to the high self-awareness, these leaders will be able to lead in uncertainty but because of their deep connection with others and through not understanding the fundamentals of team management, they may be nearing or even reaching 'burnout'.

Those leaders in the bottom left quadrant will be trundling along 'doing their best' but will probably be clumsy in their style and thus just 'getting by'. They will be likely driven by a need to be liked or be popular, which results in them avoiding tough decisions. There will come a point when they might struggle or have team members leaving.

In the bottom right quadrant are the egotistical leaders who know all the leadership models and skills and might have even won some awards. They possibly feel they are invincible and present with lots of ego. In this quadrant, the leaders will have linked their self-worth to results and outcomes. The leader I referred to in the introduction is probably here. These leaders will be afraid of showing vulnerability and believe that they must have all the answers and be right, which is not healthy in a VUCA world because their thinking will likely be blinkered.

Turning to the top right quadrant, I believe that self-awareness, when combined with leadership skills, enables the ability to lead with wisdom and authenticity. This is the space where we can sit with 'wicked' problems, without feeling inadequate when we do not have the answers or solutions. The leaders here will be centred, comfortable in their own skin and who they are as a person. They know and believe in their self-worth without having to shout about it. Therefore, they will feel comfortable asking their teams for thoughts and ideas; and as a result lead through their being rather than their doing.

Figure 1 is far from perfect as it is two-dimensional and gives the impression that self-awareness and leadership skills are of equal importance. However, this is not the case because, without self-awareness, we lack the self-knowledge of our biases, needs and motivations. And it is all these that heavily influence the how and what we do as we lead. Without full awareness of how our own belief systems, values, needs and motivations shape who we are, we will be making interventions in our lives, and the lives of others, with bias and assumption. This, to me, feels wrong in the polarized world we are living in, one which requires greater inclusivity. This links to Socrates' perspective that self-awareness is at the heart of moral and ethical leadership.

Self-connection and negative capability

How do we transition to the top right quadrant and why is developing self-awareness the route? Through self-awareness we develop greater self-connection, which is the enabler to leading and living effectively in a VUCA world. This is because self-connection is based on self-acceptance, which is characterized by being comfortable in one's own skin – perhaps a state of a settled and soothed ego, and a sense of inner calm. It's that feeling you may experience when you know in your inner being that you have done your best and that you are good enough. This is about accepting ourselves and that means *all* of ourselves, including the stuff we don't like. This is summed up beautifully by Yetunde Hofmann's quote: 'an unconditional acceptance of all of who I am as a human being' (Hofmann, 2020; p. 27). The challenge, inevitably, is the *unconditional* acceptance of our weaknesses and dark/shadow side, which we all have – we wouldn't be human otherwise. If you find this challenging to come to terms with, I think about it like a plug and remind myself that plugs can only function with a positive and negative wire. Therefore, us humans can only be whole with a positive and negative part – we just need to integrate each part into who we are. Part of this self-connection work can be aligned to what the psychologist Carl Jung described as individuation where we integrate all the parts of oneself (including the ugly parts) and get a clearer sense of self and comfort as to where we sit in the world. This includes accepting our imperfections and vulnerabilities. This will be explored further in Chapter 11.

It is this level of self-connection which facilitates the development of the capacity to lead through uncertainty, a capability described by the poet John Keats as 'negative capability'. This he defined as 'capable of being in uncertainties, mysteries, and doubts without any irritable reaching after fact and reason' (Keats, 1817). I interpret this as being comfortable with 'not knowing' and being able to embrace ambiguity. In addition, for me it is being able to sit with the discomfort of not having all the answers or not being able to make it right. This concept has also been described as 'reverie' by the psychoanalyst Wilfrid Bion (1962), which he defined as 'a mother's capacity to hold her baby's anxiety and her own, to continue thinking and offer her presence and availability without rushing too quickly to solution or leaving it too long'. In terms of leadership, this is about you accepting you don't have all the answers, that you can ask others for ideas and perspectives and that you aren't perfect – it is this humility which will underpin the capacity to lead through volatility and uncertainty. A tweet by Tom Hanks (14 Jun 23 @tomhanks), who talked about this concept, highlighted this as the 'doing of the work is the win', rather than 'the work' or the 'results' or 'outcome' being the win.

Developing this capability and capacity is about us de-latching our egos from outcomes and results, knowing that we are good enough and have stopped what Brene Brown describes as 'hustling for worthiness' (Brown, 2022). (The irony of writing and publishing a book has not escaped me!) This results in the ability to navigate and sit comfortably with the uncertain and volatile world we work in. With all this uncertainty and complexity, there is no way that, as leaders, we can possibly know what to do, or how to respond, or what intervention to use at every turn. This is about being able to sit and be comfortable with not knowing, not having the answer, holding your boundaries, accepting all your vulnerabilities, and continuing to be present with others, without clamouring after a solution or outcome. This enables better-quality thinking, and a better connection with those around you. This is a critical ingredient for today's leaders. However, this is challenging because, as leaders, we are often expected to be acting and setting a direction, but there are times as leaders when we are faced with those 'wicked problems' where there is no obvious way forward.

Therefore, the belief which would be helpful to hold on to is that the work and act of being a leader is the win. I wonder, therefore, what might become possible if you measured your leadership in terms of being rather than doing? Whilst all leaders are measured on results and outputs, the leaders that operate from the 'being' place do get results and do so with engaged teams (and are more effective leaders) – it's just often unnoticed, as these leaders tend not to shout about it!

A narcissistic activity?

It might be argued that developing self-awareness is a self-indulgent activity. In some ways it is, but if the work is done with the purpose of enhancing how you show up with others it will not be narcissistic.

For Reflection

At this juncture you might wish to ask yourself:

▸ What is the purpose for me in developing self-awareness, and how might it benefit my leadership?

Hard work is in store

I am hoping that you are starting to appreciate why self-awareness is important and that it might be worthwhile investing some effort and focus on developing it. However, it is not an easy process. There will be times when you will be struggling to do this work, and you may hear the voice of your 'inner critic' increase in volume and even begin to derail you. For years, self-awareness was perceived to be a negative and aversive state of mind because it led to rumination, possibly anxiety and depression. With that in mind, I invite you to take this work on as a reflective practice, noticing, highlighting and underlining the strengths, sparkles and positives, and, above all, be compassionate to yourself. When you hit those darker moments and the loud inner critic emerges, or your uglies get louder please seek support, rather than slip into rumination. I have valued working with a therapist, a thinking partner, and coaches, in conjunction with activities that build my resilience, such as regular yoga and exercise.

> **For Reflection**
>
> When I am working with leaders in this space, I ask them (each of these questions needs an honest answer for them to be of value):
>
> ▶ Who can support you in this work?
>
> ▶ How will you resource yourself to do the work?
>
> ▶ How will you hold yourself accountable for doing the work?

Too self-aware?

There has been some debate posed on social media as to whether one can be 'too self-aware'. To dispel that myth, as highlighted above, self-awareness is a dynamic construct that is ever evolving. The 'too much' possibly occurs when one stops being reflective and compassionate and tips into rumination, self-flagellation and possibly becomes depressed – this could be perceived as 'too much' self-awareness. Therefore, to repeat what was stated above, do this work with self-compassion and curiosity and be kind to yourself.

In finishing this Chapter, I just want to be clear that I am not believing for one moment I have reached this space yet, and I continue to focus hard on self-acceptance, of *all* of who I am as a human being (including the bits I don't like). Self-awareness for all of us is a never-ending and infinite game.

> **For Reflection**
>
> Before moving to the next chapter, take a moment to reflect on:
>
> - How self-aware do you believe you are now?
> - How might developing it support you in your role as a leader or coach?
> - What is resonating with you? And what are you disagreeing with?
> - What support might you need on this journey? What support have you got in place?

Further Resources

If you want to read more about the nature of infinite games this is a helpful resource:

- Carse, J. (2011). *Finite and infinite games.* Simon and Schuster.

Chapter 2
So, you think you know what self-awareness is

> 'He who knows others is wise; he who knows himself is enlightened.'
> Lao Tzu, c.604–c.531 BC

When I started researching self-awareness I was under the illusion, because it was so widely talked about and mentioned, as were the claims about what it led to, that it was going to be a well-defined construct. This illusion was quickly dispelled when I began delving into the literature and research! As I highlighted in Chapter 1, self-awareness is a complex construct that has, up until recently, been poorly defined in the adult and leadership development space. It is frequently confused with other concepts such as self-consciousness and self-knowledge. Therefore, the aim of this chapter is to offer you some clarity and a definition as to what self-awareness is and how it differs from self-consciousness and self-knowledge. This will give you a starting point in terms of thinking about your own self-awareness and identifying areas to start working on. In essence, we cannot develop self-awareness if we do not know what it is, and furthermore, all the ingredients of which it comprises.

It is, therefore, not surprising that self-awareness is misunderstood when we unpick the meaning of firstly self, and then awareness. Each of these elements in themselves are hard to grasp and get a sense of, as there are so many different lenses we can explore them through – taking such approaches as philosophical, psychological, spiritual or sociological. I am not going to attempt to tackle all these perspectives here. Instead, my aim is to give you a simple, practical definition that you can grasp and work with rather than getting overwhelmed by the meaning of 'self' and its mass of interpretations. However, you may like to reflect on whether you are drawn to philosophical, psychological, spiritual, sociological or practical perspectives as this will provide you with some data about your thinking patterns and the beliefs that underpin these.

To be clear about how I perceive self and then awareness as a basis for my definition, I have taken the view that the self and awareness are multi-dimensional and multi-layered in nature. The self is made up of conscious and unconscious aspects and is informed by others' observations. This is because we are relational beings and social animals who cannot exist in isolation, as we are wired for connection. Similarly, awareness is multi-faceted and is based on the recognition of our own feelings, how others feel and our impact on others.

Self-awareness is a complex, multi-layered construct made up of several individual components, or, as I like to call them, ingredients. Subsequent chapters will take each of these ingredients individually and explore them in greater depth. The definition of self-awareness, which comes from my research, is:

> *'Self-Awareness is a range of inter-personal (the perception of others and individual behaviours) and intra-personal components (beliefs, values, strengths, weaknesses, motivations, internal mental state and physiological responses) which when developed underpin self and connection with others'.*

This is a somewhat wordy definition and to make this easier to understand, I have presented the definition visually below:

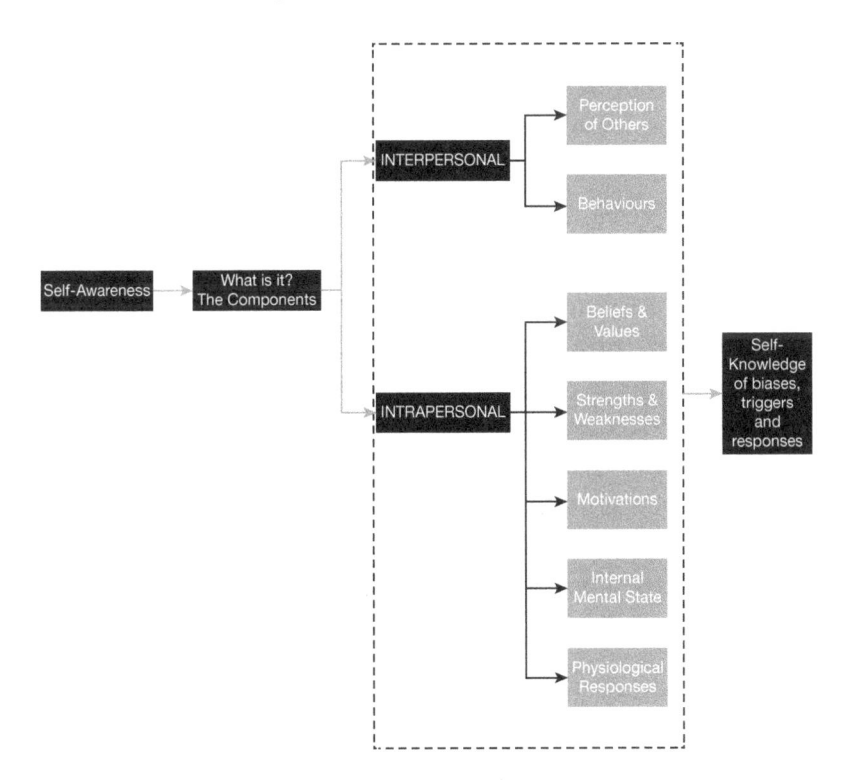

Figure 2: The components of self-awareness

The ingredients of self-awareness

I prefer the word 'ingredients' because a cake without the ingredients required in the recipe just doesn't taste or even look as good as one in which all ingredients are added. It is my fervent belief that we need all the ingredients in order to be truly self-aware. All the ingredients require work, and each one is worthy of dedicated time and effort. As you will see in Figure 2, the ingredients are clustered under one of two over-arching components of either inter-personal or intra-personal.

The inter-personal ingredients are placed first, at the top and forefront, because we are talking about being self-aware for the purpose of being effective as leaders and coaches. These ingredients are about developing an awareness of how we are in relation to others. This is about connecting and relating to others, and as leading is a relational business, it makes sense we start here. The intra-personal ingredients focus on our own internal awareness of resources, frame of mind and feelings; the introspective elements.

To support you in thinking about what I mean by inter-personal and intra-personal, the Johari Window concept is helpful. The Johari Window was developed by psychologists Joseph and Harrington Ingham in the 1950s as a framework for understanding relationship with self and others (Luft and Ingham, 1955). It identifies what is known to self (individuals) and what is known about us by others. The inter-personal ingredients are 'known by others', and the intra-personal ones are 'known to self'.

Whilst the diagram in Figure 2 presents the ingredients as being discrete and individual it is rather messier than that! In essence, the ingredients are inter-related and often one might drive another; therefore, working on one is likely to give us insight to another. Subsequent Chapters take each ingredient at a time, and I start with the inter-personal components. However, you might prefer to start at a different point, for example, internal mental state (Chapter 9) and that work might reveal some new insights around behaviours (Chapter 5) or beliefs and values (Chapter 6); or you might start with beliefs and values and that will reveal something about your behaviours or physiological responses. With that in mind, you may choose to start with an ingredient you are particularly interested in and come back to the others at a later stage. If you are unsure where to start, I recommend starting with beliefs and values, since getting clear on these is a good starting point for finding inner peace.

A leader of an SME, who I was working with, found that becoming clear on her values was fundamental in helping her decide on the direction she wished to take the business. There are many ways of doing this work and I will expand on this in Parts 2 and 3.

It was at this point in my research, when I had defined self-awareness, that I realized I perhaps had not been developing it effectively, as up until then I had no comprehension of the complexity or the detail of how it was made up. This is why we are not as self-aware as we may think. Moreover, self-awareness is dynamic in nature, and it evolves, ebbs and flows. Importantly, there is no measure of it per se which reinforces the view that we can never say we are self-aware, or that we are done!

How do self-consciousness and self-knowledge differ from self-awareness?

Self-consciousness and self-knowledge are either part of, or linked to self-awareness, and whilst the terms might be used interchangeably, the differentiation is discussed below to provide clarity for you to consider. The greatest overlap between self-awareness and self-consciousness occurs when we study it from an intra-personal perspective. Self-consciousness is largely categorized and defined from an intra-personal angle, although there are some writers who add in the interpersonal element. This, to my mind, is too confusing. To be clear and establish some parameters, self-consciousness is limited to the intra-personal dimension of self-awareness in my definition. Therefore, by developing these ingredients you will be developing self-consciousness, such that it is an integral part of self-awareness.

Turning to self-knowledge. Self-knowledge has been defined as 'accurate self-perceptions about how one typically thinks, feels and behaves, and awareness of how these patterns are interpreted by others' (Vazire and Carlson, 2010; p. 606). The question is how do you develop these perceptions? Drawing on Figure 2 they are developed through self-awareness. Therefore, self-knowledge is the result or output of self-awareness, because it leads to knowledge of your biases, triggers and responses. This is perhaps why the American psychologist and science journalist, Daniel Goleman (2021), who has researched and written about emotional intelligence, saw self-awareness as a key tenet of emotional intelligence.

In sum, self-consciousness is the intra-personal dimension of self-awareness, and thus, it is an element or part of it. Whereas self-knowledge is the result and output of developing it. This means that through working on developing your self-awareness, you will also be developing self-consciousness and self-knowledge.

The next chapter will explore what we need to do to develop self-awareness and how to start the work, before taking each component in turn in subsequent chapters. However, by getting clear on what self-awareness is, the work has already started.

> **Before moving to the next chapter, take a moment to reflect**
>
> These questions will start to give you some insight into how you make meaning and what informs your thinking. As you look at these questions, notice your initial response, your feelings, your thoughts and physiological responses – all of this is part of developing self-awareness.
>
> - How would you define self-awareness?
>
> - As you look at the definition above – what are you attracted to? What do you disagree with? What don't you like?
>
> - Looking at Figure 2, what are your initial thoughts on each of the ingredients? Which ones do you believe you need to pay attention to?

Further Resources

If you wish to read the academic research behind this concept, look at the published systematic literature review which is the basis of the definitions offered in this Chapter.

- Carden, J., Jones, R. J. & Passmore, J. (2022). Defining self-awareness in the context of adult development: A systematic literature review in *Journal of Management Education*, 46 (1), 140–177.

Chapter 3
Doing the work: where to start?

'There are no shortcuts to any place worth going'
Anon

Gaining an understanding and clarity of what self-awareness is, represents the first stage in developing it. The next stage is to get motivated and interested in doing the work, because, as I highlighted in Chapter 1, this work is not always easy. It is imperative that you are purposeful and motivated to do the work otherwise your self-awareness will not be developed. Therefore, a starting point is to perhaps explore your motivation to develop it.

For Reflection

Below are some reflective questions to help you understand your motivation to develop self-awareness:

- How might doing this work benefit a) me as a human soul and b) my leadership?

- What will I gain if I do this work? How will this be of benefit to a) my team; b) my organization; c) my stakeholders and d) my other relationships?

- What might I lose if I don't do the work?

- How will I keep my 'feet to the fire' so that I avoid storytelling, self-delusion or self-deception?

- How will I know I am making progress? (Do consider that slipping backwards, losing ground and wallowing in one place can also be perceived as progress).

- How motivated am I to do this work (on a scale of 1–10, with 10 being highly motivated)? If less than 9 or 10, what needs to happen/shift/change to increase my motivation?

Just taking time to reflect on your responses to the questions above will start to give you some data and information that can feed into the evolution of your self-awareness. By paying attention to how you are feeling and responding to the questions posed throughout this book, you will be gaining new insights and will be developing self-awareness as you go!

Warning: what capacity do you have to do this work?

We can be highly motivated to do this work, have identified a purpose and be fully committed but we just may not have the capacity to engage. What do I mean by capacity? I am talking about headspace, the mental and physical well-being necessary to hold or contain what is emerging. Therefore, think about your capacity before you start.

> **For Reflection**
>
> ▶ To what extent have I got the capacity and resilience to do this work right now?
>
> ▶ What can I tolerate?

Reflecting on these questions will support us in deciding what we engage in, because there will be times when we can undertake multiple activities, go deep and bare our souls; and there are also times when we are feeling less resilient and small moments are enough. However, watch out at this point as you might be giving yourself a way out – so notice if your response is something like: 'I haven't got time, and therefore, I haven't got the capacity; thank you Julia – you have just given me an excuse not to do the work!' My challenge to you in response to this is that time is not an excuse and, by having this response, I am curious as to 'what are you avoiding?' Of course, you may well slip into some justifiable rationalization as to why you haven't got either the time or capacity but do please pause and challenge yourself and be curious as to what you might be avoiding or running away from. I say this because if you are motivated then you will find the time. I often experience this 'lack of time' with senior leaders who struggle to find and commit to the time for coaching – this of course may not be due to wanting to avoid something, but it may well be!

The next stage: self-questioning

Having got clear on what self-awareness is and assessed your motivation to do the work, the next stage is to initiate some self-questioning, from a position of learning, growth and kindness. Nancy Kline (2009) highlights in her *Time to Think* work that we all think better in the presence of a question, so identify some questions that will support you in doing this work. Posing a question to self will also initiate unconscious work alongside the things we are consciously focusing on; it's as if it is percolating through our very being and whole self. These questions might be bigger questions, for example what is my purpose?; or what is the contribution I wish to make? Alternatively, the questions could be linked to one of the individual components of self-awareness, such as what is the unmet need in me that I am meeting through my work?; or which of my core beliefs underpin my leadership?; or, as discussed with one leader, what are the beliefs which are getting in the way?

Start getting curious as to why you are behaving, thinking, feeling, responding and acting in the way you are – this curiosity will serve you well in driving you to be open to learning more about yourself. A helpful question to ask yourself in this space is:

- Why am I behaving/feeling/thinking in the way I am?
- Where might that/this stem from?

At this stage, maybe take a moment to identify some questions for yourself. Equally, I encourage you to do this in relation to each of the core components as you read through the chapters. I often ask groups that I am working with to think about: 'what is the question you are taking from today which will support your development of self-awareness?' Questions are powerful in this space.

How to do the work?

Firstly, the development of self-awareness is a very personal journey and there is no one way of developing it. Nor can we develop it by doing one thing once and then be done, as it is a dynamic construct which is ever evolving. Instead, we must engage in a myriad of activities which, when combined, will form the whole. I like to think about it as several jigsaw pieces that when successfully connected, form the whole picture and deepen our self-awareness. As you go on to read subsequent Chapters about each of the ingredients, you will begin to identify the pieces of your own jigsaw, which will feed into your own development. Figure 3 is the result of my research, which explored how coaches develop self-awareness. The pieces represent the activities that are engaged in to develop it, where the larger pieces highlight a theme, and the smaller pieces are individual activities supporting that theme. For example, for coaches, some form of experiential learning, which included doing some coaching, was important. Your themes and individual activities are unlikely to be the same. However, based on experience and research, reflection and experiential based activities are central to the development of self-awareness, so perhaps think about what might feed into this space for you.

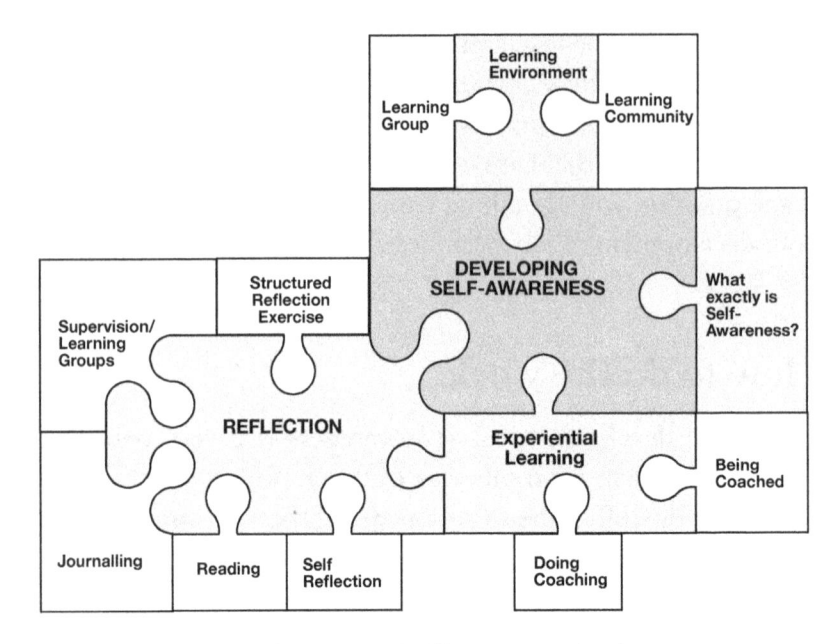

Figure 3: The jigsaw of self-awareness development

In thinking about the activities you engage in, you may find it worthwhile to think about your own preferences and your preferred learning styles, as these will help shape what you participate in. If you are interested in exploring this further have a look at Honey and Mumford Learning Styles questionnaire (Honey and Mumford, 1982); there are several free versions on the internet. There are no absolutes with these questionnaires and many educational psychologists suggest that there is no evidence to underpin these styles (Pashler et al, 2008). However, they can provide you with a starting point which you might not be able to access in other ways.

A word of caution about questionnaires/inventories

There is a myriad of personality profiles, learning style questionnaires and the like available either free or for a charge that all claim to develop self-awareness. They can provide a piece of the jigsaw, but only one small piece – they are not conclusive or definitive. Therefore, please treat them with caution and as a piece of data and information rather than *the* answer, or as a definitive answer to you and your self-awareness. They really are just *a* piece of the jigsaw. Therefore, if you do undertake completing one (or several) of these profiles and questionnaires, take time to notice and ask yourself the following so that the outcome can support you:

- How do I feel about the results/outcome of the profile/questionnaire?
- What do I agree with? What am I assuming is the *truth*?
- What do I disagree with?
- What other evidence have I got to support or question the data/information?

Reflection: *essential* to developing self-awareness

You will notice in Figure 3 that 'reflection' is a large and sizable piece of the jigsaw; this is because engaging in reflection is a primary means of developing self-awareness, which was also fundamental to the philosophy of Socrates. In terms of self-awareness, engaging in reflection is non-negotiable. Doing an activity without reflection is unlikely to deepen your self-awareness, because as highlighted by Kolb (1984) in his learning cycle theory, it is the reflection and integration of that reflection post an experience/activity which results in your learning. This means that when you are doing something in your business that is high stakes or new, take some time to reflect afterwards.

Case Study

I once worked with a senior leader who wished to have greater impact in a team meeting. Having identified some new strategies to try out I encouraged reflection on completion of the meeting with the following questions:

- What did I try today?
- What went well? What did I do well?
- What am I going to do differently next time?

In terms of self-awareness, it would also be beneficial to add:

- What am I learning about myself?

It was the leader's reflection, after trying out the new strategy, which led to new insight and ways of behaving.

Of course, I am conscious that reflection is not a natural preference for everyone and you may be one of those who hate doing it. In addition, our modern life in terms of pace, always being connected and 'switched on' does not create an environment which is conducive to reflection! However, those 'who care deeply about their work need to commit to creating the space for reflective practice' (Van Nieuwerburgh and Love, 2025; p. 11). Therefore, to assist you and before you read on it might be useful to stop and think about your relationship to reflection.

> **For Reflection**
>
> ▸ What does reflection mean to you?
> ▸ What do I think it involves?
> ▸ How do I feel about engaging in reflection?
> ▸ What don't I like about reflection?

You may feel that reflection is about being still, silent and alone and you don't like these sorts of activities. Therefore, let me bust some myths.

Busting myths about reflection

Reflection can be done with others

Whether this is with one other person or as a group, reflection does not need to be a solitary activity. I do much of my reflection with others as I engage in weekly therapy, monthly thinking sessions with a thinking partner, monthly sessions with my coaching supervisor and a 6–8 weekly group supervision session (supervision is a reflective practice for coaches, which could also be used in leadership). However, in the spirit of developing your self-awareness as you read, here are some questions to reflect on.

> **For Reflection**
>
> ▸ What is it about being alone that I dislike?
> ▸ What does being solitary mean I will need/have to tackle?
> ▸ What am I avoiding by doing this work with others?

Reflection must be done in silence

You may find it helpful talking through your reflections or having music playing to inspire reflection. However, if you dislike silence, I do encourage you to think about it.

> **For Reflection**
> - What is it that I don't like about silence?
> - What is the silence representing/meaning to me?
> - What do I have to confront in the silence that I am avoiding?

For many of us, silence and stillness mean we must confront ourselves fully in a space where we can't run away – this can be a scary place!

Reflection will take time

Dedicated reflection time is important, and that's why being with others can help, as we are committed to them and that can force us or give us the dedicated time to do it. However, a few minutes when we catch a glimpse, have a realization or gain an insight are just as valuable. I believe that once we have become motivated to do the work and initiated some self-questioning, we are increasingly likely to gain these 'glimpses'. Therefore, if you are time-short, maybe just commit to a few moments each day or week where you think about 'what have you learnt about yourself' or to 'pose yourself a new question to hold for the next week or so?' You could ask yourself the following questions.

> **For Reflection**
> - What has emerged for me today/this week?
> - What's the question or headline I am now taking to continue my thinking/work on this?

Personal perception of reflection

For me, reflection is about stepping back and pausing alone or with another person – I like a combination as it is often revealing and motivating with others. I prefer to do this in a more formalized way, and I need to dedicate and commit to it, which means I need to book time in my schedule. Then again, the informal, unscheduled reflections that I gain on a dog-walk or doing something else are also of value. I find the moments of space and stillness invaluable. It is in those moments where time slows down and there is some silence, that I can capture glimpses of my unconscious and deepen my understanding of 'why I am behaving in the way I am'. Personally, I was guilty of saying 'I've not got the time for this' which, when combined with my preference for being busy, doing and action, meant that doing reflection and being reflective did not come naturally to me. Therefore, it has taken me some time to fall in love with doing it, but I know, based on both my research and my experience, that reflection and reflective activities are critical to the development of self-awareness.

Methods of reflection

There are so many methods for reflecting with or without others and I do not wish to be prescriptive as I don't believe one activity is of more value than another. What works for me is committed time with others (e.g. thinking time with a thinking partner), journalling as thoughts/feelings arise, or when I am triggered in some way, walking in nature – normally talking to my dogs as I go (I like to extrovert my thinking) and doing yoga. I have also tried other activities, for example, love and kindness meditation, and gratitude journalling. Other activities might include (this is not an exhaustive list, but just some ideas):

- Mind-mapping
- Drawing
- A retreat/silent retreat
- Daily questions
- Pause moments
- Reading or writing poetry or a haiku
- Reading

Journalling

I indicate that journalling is a useful technique throughout this book, and you will be introduced to some methods of doing this, e.g. free-fall writing (Chapter 7) and gratitude journalling (Chapter 11). However, it can take many forms, and I encourage you to be creative, try different ways and find something that works for you. Journalling might also be in the form of mind-mapping, drawing, cartooning, writing a poem or a haiku (a short, unrhymed poem, typically with five syllables in the first line, seven in the second and five in the third). It can be structured or unstructured. My preference is to do this by hand in a small journal notebook, rather than on a tablet or PC, and a few tips from my experience:

- Write unfiltered – capture whatever comes up as this is what might enable you to gain glimpses of your unconscious.

- Spelling and grammar are irrelevant in this space.
- Capture feelings as well as thoughts.
- Note a date (this will enable you to track themes and development).
- Generate questions (which can be left unanswered – your unconscious will percolate them if you leave them in the ether).
- Make links and connections.
- Maybe set a timer and write for a set amount of time.
- Avoid just recounting what happened and the facts, instead write about what is coming up for you and what meaning you are making from whatever you are reflecting on.

Remember that whatever you write will be right, it is yours and no-one else need ever see or read it.

If you are new in this space and want some support, I have made some recommendations at the end of the chapter in the 'further resources' section.

Where to start?

Once we have got clarity as to what self-awareness is, identified our motivation and initiated some self-questioning, it can feel somewhat overwhelming to find a place to start. If you are struggling to identify a starting point or are thinking I am already doing this work and wondering where to go next, it is helpful to go back to Figure 2 and look at the components. Use this figure to identify which of the components you perhaps have not done any work on or have neglected and perhaps start there. For example, after I had developed this visual representation of self-awareness, I realized I had not spent enough time getting to really know and understand my physiological responses (I spend way too much time in my head and unsurprisingly for someone who engages in academia put more value on the cognitive elements of self-awareness). This led to me engaging a somatic specialist as my coaching supervisor, booking a yoga retreat and reading more about my physical being (I can recommend James Nestor's book *Breath* (Nestor, 2021). In sum, start by using Figure 2 and reviewing the ingredients. You might perhaps subjectively assess how self-aware you are in relation to each of the individual components and choose the one you rate the lowest as a starting point; or like me, identify the one you have paid the least attention. If that fails, I recommend you start with values and beliefs (Chapter 6) because this can provide insight to many of the other ones. Don't be fooled into thinking this is a shortcut to self-awareness, because this is a challenging component to work on and can require some soul-searching!

Final words on doing the work

I have already highlighted above that this work can be challenging and uncomfortable, and, in those moments of challenge and discomfort, we can allow our ego defences to take over and move to denial, justification and storytelling. During my early research days, an academic tutor posed the question 'self-awareness or self-delusion' and pointed me in the direction of David Owen's book *Hubris* (Owen, 2012). There is more on this in Chapter 12. We are naturally wired to hear and see what we want to see and hear, and none of us want to see and hear the full picture all the time, so it is easy to slip into storytelling and justification. Therefore, it is important that we are mindful of self-delusion (failing to recognize reality) or self-deception (denying or rationalizing away the relevance, significance or importance of evidence, or viewpoints that are contradictory to what we believe and feel or what we want to believe and feel). With that in mind, start noticing when you are slipping into denial, disagreeing and justifying – this can be in the moment or at a later point. Be curious as to what you might either been protecting or defending in yourself. The storytelling, self-deception and self-delusion are all perfectly normal human traits, which we all do all the time, and we can't stop ourselves doing so, as our unconscious will always act to keep us safe. However, what we can do is start noticing it and undertaking some self-questioning. In my experience, those painful, agonizing moments when something is revealed to us that we don't like or find uncomfortable, are the gold nuggets of self-discovery. However, we can only stand in those moments if we have the resilience and capacity to do so and we have the support we need.

Lastly, please remember that we never reach being 100% self-aware because it is a dynamic, ever-evolving construct which ebbs and flows. Nevertheless, every piece of work we do will deepen our understanding and awareness, and over time we become increasingly self-aware both consciously and unconsciously.

For Reflection

Before moving to the next chapter, take a moment to reflect:

- Think about times when you have been 'triggered' – what might that experience open to you?
- What would be the most difficult aspect of self for you to reflect on?

Coming up

Chapters 4 to 10 tackle each of the ingredients of self-awareness individually. Each Chapter will give you a description of the component, thoughts on how to develop it and finish with more questions to support your development in this area. For all the ingredients, working with a coach and/or therapist can be an effective way of gaining insight and developing it. Whilst Figure 2 (in Chapter 2) and these Chapters indicate each component is distinct and separate, it is not actually as black and white as that, and as I highlighted above, they are all inter-linked and intertwined. For example, our values and beliefs often underpin how we are behaving or feeling in a situation or context, and often by exploring one aspect we will gain valuable data about another component – so do keep an open mind as to what is emerging and what you are learning. This can make the work messy and unstructured, so whilst you might choose one component to focus on developing be prepared to gain more awareness about others and this is an outcome that may very well shock you.

Further Resources

These are some resources which can support you in exploring how to write reflectively and different methods for reflection. I have also included James Nestor's *Breath* to explore some of the physiological aspects of self-awareness.

- Bolton, G. (2018 – 5th Edn). *Reflective practice: Writing & professional development.* SAGE Publications Limited.

- Lucas, M. (2023). *Creating the reflective habit: A practical guide for coaches, mentors and leaders.* Routledge.

- Nestor, J. (2021). *Breath.* Penguin Life.

- van Nieuwerburgh, C. & Love, D. (2025). *Your essential guide to effective reflective practice: Improving practice through self-reflection and writing.* SAGE Publications Limited.

PART 2
SELF-AWARENESS: INTRODUCING THE INTER-PERSONAL COMPONENTS

Introducing the inter-personal components

> *'How do others see and experience us?'*
> Author, 2025

As we are doing this work in service of leading and working with others, it feels important to start with the elements of self-awareness which are about how others experience us and our impact on others with regard to the inter-personal elements. These are the components that others see and are observed in relation with others, what Tasha Eurich refers to as 'external self-awareness', that is, 'knowing how other people see you' (Eurich, 2017; p. 8). However, getting to grips with these aspects of self-awareness is the most challenging work, because it is reliant on input from those who we interact with. In addition, we are faced with the question as to how accurate their input will be, because they could easily be projecting their own stuff onto us, or perhaps even idolizing us. In addition, possibly through their avoidance of tension and a need to be liked, they just don't provide us with a full, honest and transparent picture, which is the important stuff we really need to hear.

In addition, we must also be open and grounded to receive what those around us might share with us so that we can integrate it into our awareness. This is of course related to our personal capacity as discussed in Chapter 3, so with that in mind it is important that we only work on these elements when we are mentally in the right place to receive and act upon what is being said.

Thinking traps and distortions

As highlighted in Chapter 3, we must be cognisant of our natural tendencies for storytelling, denial and avoidance. I know that when I am tired, not feeling on top form or struggling with life-stuff, I resort to avoiding, ignoring or justifying. Therefore, managing your own well-being, finding space and being compassionate to self are also part of the work. To support you in avoiding self-delusion and self-deception, it might be helpful to notice what thinking distortions and traps you might fall into, which will get in the way of deepening your self-awareness. The concept of 'thinking traps and distortions' comes from cognitive behavioural therapy and coaching and some are listed below. As you read these, try to identify the ones you tend to fall into. I once was working with a leader who quickly identified he tended to slip into nearly all these thinking traps a great deal of the time. This awareness benefitted his leadership style and as a result he consciously made some changes when he delegated. Once you are aware of the traps, start noticing if you are slipping into one of them as you are learning about how others perceive you.

Thinking traps and distortions to be aware of when thinking about the inter-personal components:

- *Mind-Reading:* This might be when you catch yourself saying 'I knew that person thought I was useless'; or 'I knew they would challenge me on the pay-plan.'

- *Fortune Telling:* When you start predicting what might happen by saying 'I know they aren't going to say anything favorable.'

- *Black and White thinking:* When you only see polarized perspectives rather than a range of possibilities. When you receive one comment out of several that is negative and then adopt the stance of 'this is all bad.'

- *Filtering:* When you might only focus on the bad or the good. Are you someone who pushes aside or diminishes positive feedback and comments?

- *Labelling:* is a form of generalization when you take a generalization, for example, 'everyone thinks I am useless' and then you label yourself in a critical way with 'I'm just not good enough'.

- *Shoulds/Oughts:* The 'shoulds' and 'oughts' will be linked to beliefs you have about yourself. This thinking distortion will lead you quickly towards thinking something like 'I should just be better' and entering a mindset of self-flagellation rather than really processing what you are receiving. The beliefs are often based on something we learnt as a child.

- *Always being right:* When you take the other person's feedback and rationalize or justify it by making yourself right and going on to say, 'I was only doing/saying that because___'

How do we develop the inter-personal components?

For me to dig deep into these aspects, I need to receive feedback, inputs and perspectives from those whom I trust, and whom I believe are both credible and competent. Alongside this, I need to be in a good place mentally, feeling resilient and importantly grounded. Therefore, I urge you to think about who you ask and what you need, so that you can receive and process what you are hearing or reading. I find it helpful to journal, noting what has been said, how I feel as I receive the information, noting my responses and later feelings and then sitting down with my therapist, a coach or coaching supervisor to reflect on what has been said. You may find the reflective questions below a helpful starting point.

For Reflection

Before moving to the next chapter, take a moment to reflect:

- ▸ Who can you bear to hear saying what needs to be said, but which you would rather not hear?

- ▸ Who do you know who will be most honest with you, who will be courageous in what they are saying?

- ▸ How will you know you have the capacity and resilience to receive what is being said?

- ▸ What conditions will create the safety for you to absorb what you are hearing?

- ▸ If you do slip into storytelling – what is the story you are telling yourself? What might you learn about yourself from this story?

The inter-personal components are:

- ▸ Others' Perceptions – Chapter 4
- ▸ Behaviours – Chapter 5

Chapter 4
Developing self-awareness: the inter-personal component of others' perceptions

> 'There are things known and there are things unknown, and in between are the doors of perception.'
> Aldous Huxley, 1954

This component relates to how you are perceived and received by others including what they see and hear you doing, and how they feel when they are with you. It is also about the relationships we create and maintain, and the unconscious dynamics in those relationships, which when identified will present us with greater insight. As the psychoanalyst Manfred Kets De Vries (2014) says: 'the space between people is filled with what we evoke in one another', and as a leader getting an appreciation of what we are evoking in our teams is important. This component is about having an awareness of oneself through the eyes of others. It has been highlighted (Carden et al, 2022b; Rochat, 2018) that having a sense of how others 'evaluate' or assess us can benefit your self-awareness. I use the term 'assess' because the reality is we are all making assessments and judgements of others all the time – our brains are doing it naturally. It is how others are evaluating and assessing you in relation to themselves; and critically this is of course based on their own individual 'map of their world', their filters, and their level of resilience in that moment. As highlighted in the introduction, this is what makes developing this component so very challenging and why we never attain full self-awareness!

> **Case Study**
>
> I was once working with a leader who wanted his team to see him in a certain way; his questions to me were around 'how can I make them___?' The trap in this perspective was that he thought he could make his team see him in a certain light or control their feelings. However, you cannot make anyone feel in a certain way when they are around you. The key was to explore how he was behaving, and what was driving those behaviours all of which were in his gift to control and change.

Methods for developing this component

Below are a variety of methods in support of developing this aspect.

Seeking Feedback

Before I talk about seeking feedback, I just want to pause and consider the emotive word that is 'feedback' – it is a word and action which naturally triggers defensiveness and wariness. It almost certainly causes the brain's primal survival responses of fight, flight or freeze and it will undoubtedly elicit thinking distortions! Therefore, maybe reframe by thinking about it as data. Perhaps ask for data or information about yourself instead of using the term feedback. Remember it is like personality profiles – it is just a piece of the jigsaw; and it is not the absolute truth. Again, be mindful of storytelling, rationalization and justification.

Working with a coach can be invaluable as coaches can often and more easily give you the feedback that your team and subordinates can't. This may be something to ask of your coach – how are they experiencing you? You might also ask them to offer their feelings and perceptions on the things you talk about during your coaching sessions. During a coaching session with a leader who was outlining how they would be running a strategic away-weekend with their top team, they started going through all the PowerPoint slides they had prepared. As they were doing this, I was becoming increasingly bored, felt no connection to the leader or what they were trying to portray, so I reflected this back and said, 'I find myself getting bored and switching off; I wonder if your team might feel the same on a Friday night?' The first response was a defensive reaction, naturally, but by the end of the session they said, 'thank you for the challenge, nobody else would have said that to me.'

Think about asking a mix of people such as peers, team members, friends, family members and acquaintances, with regard to how they feel in your presence, and what your impact is upon them. Maybe give them the chance to reflect on this and write their thoughts, as they may feel safer and more secure doing it that way. To maximize the utility of this work, it is very worthwhile to think about doing some 'contracting' around this exercise. What do I mean by the word contracting in this context? Being clear on why you are seeking the feedback, and what you will be doing with it. Perhaps explore how you might ask some follow-up questions, and what to do if either you or the other party start to feel discomfort. Once you have done some contracting, be clear and specific on the questions you ask. For example, 'what do you think of me?' is too broad a question and somewhat confrontational in nature. Instead ask something specific. There are some example questions below.

Possible questions to ask others:

- What do I do that you appreciate? And what do I do that irritates you? (do ask both!)
- What have I done that has been of value?
- What do I do that motivates you?
- What would have made our time together of more value/benefit?
- How do you feel when you are with me? (Avoid – how do I *make* you feel, because we own and choose our feelings.) Or how do you feel in my presence? What do I/can I do that changes these feelings?
- How do you find my tone of voice or my pace of delivery?
- In what situations do you notice me become animated? How is that for you when I am like that?

Receiving the feedback

It is important you think about how you will receive the feedback; some of us find receiving positive feedback as uncomfortable as the more critical feedback (notice your preference regarding this). When receiving the feedback, notice your response as this is useful data about you, but do not respond from this place; instead take a breath, acknowledge what you have heard and thank the other person, letting them know you will reflect on it. To let them know you have heard, try to reflect back using the same words the other person used; this will show them you heard what they had to say. This is challenging, but this is our edge where we can develop – remembering that many believe we do not learn unless we step into a brave space which is a little out of our comfort zone. You will feel vulnerable – that's inevitable but as Brene Brown (2015) highlights, there is no bravery without vulnerability. If you need further clarity or wish to deepen understanding of the other person's feedback, ask follow-up questions from a 'seeking to understand perspective' rather than one that is to sooth your ego or justify yourself!

Once you have received some feedback, reflect on how you will process and integrate it; this might be through journalling (see Chapter 3) and personal reflection with a coach, a therapist or a thinking partner. Throughout this process remember that the feedback is simply information, provided at a moment in time and will, to some extent, be dependent on the other person and what is going on in their world. Whilst this is not an excuse to 'ditch it', do remember to treat what you are hearing with acceptance, acknowledgement and, most importantly, hold it lightly with compassion for self. You might find it supportive to hold yourself with unconditional positive regard knowing that you are a whole, resourceful human being that does not need to be fixed.

Reflection post receiving feedback

Before I reflect on a recent experience of myself seeking and receiving feedback, I will just give you some context about my 'inner workings'. One of my core values is competence; for most of my school and adult life, I have been striving to be 'good enough' and with this I have a loud 'inner critic', which sounds like a grating squawky parrot in my head. This means that I can be critical of others as much as I am critical of myself. This was highlighted to me by Robin Shohet when I was on a course with him and reflecting on how my inner critic can sometimes sabotage my learning. Robin said 'yes, I notice there's a critical energy about you, and your warm smile attempts to hide it' – this was like a slap in the face. Whilst I wanted to deny that I have a critical energy and desperately wanted affirmation from others that I am not perceived as Robin described, it proved a valuable piece of feedback that really led to me being in touch with a lack of self-acceptance and highlighted the development work I needed to do.

Recently, I was reviewing and reflecting on a supervisory relationship with one of my supervisees. I had signposted to her before the session that I thought it might be healthy to check in on how our supervision relationship was working. During our review, my supervisee highlighted that she was finding the supervision valuable, and she looks forward to the sessions. I then explored 'what would make the sessions even more valuable?' After some further reflection and probing around levels of challenge, my supervisee said that there were a couple of times I may have been a 'bit too challenging', and because she perceives me as being more experienced than her 'she felt tested'. You can imagine how this unleashed the squawky parrot in my head, but also feelings of shame; every ounce of me wanted to jump in, apologise and make it better. Instead, I placed my feet flat on the floor and explored when this might happen and how we could catch this in the future. In reflection with her, we identified that she valued the directness and challenge but that I could make it more impactful if I slowed down a little and thereby make it feel gentler. We agreed to play with this. Where has this taken me in terms of my self-awareness and what have I learnt? I have learnt that when my thoughts flow into my head, my energy picks up and, in my urgency, my critical energy is possibly revealed. So, slowing down can not only support my presence and sense of being grounded, it can also change the way I impact others.

Keep a log of how others respond and react in your presence

Start noticing how others respond to you in different moments and contexts – noticing how they react to you in terms of body language, voice (tone, volume and pace) and words they use. Keep a record of these responses and then do a review so as to identify any patterns and standouts. Having done this, try and identify the themes and patterns that are emerging, and what might these tell you about you? You might find it helpful to do this over a fixed period or during a certain project/assignment. When doing this work, it is important you note the context and what else is happening in the wider system; you can then also track if the patterns change in different contexts. Through this you will also become aware of how the system is shaping and influencing how you are showing up.

360-degree feedback

The more common way of collecting data and assessments on how others are perceiving you is through 360-degree feedback. There are many tools on the market that can support you in doing this, with a variety of focus areas such as emotional intelligence. Alternatively, you can design your own – focusing on specific areas you wish to receive feedback on; these might be leadership competencies or strengths and weaknesses to name but two. The challenge here will be to pick a broad range of respondents and to challenge yourself to choose some who you would prefer not to ask! To avoid any bias and self-delusion, it might be beneficial for a neutral party or a coach to analyse the data and present it to you. There have been many leaders and managers who have brought their 360 results into a coaching session, and often there is something surprising to unpick. I am always curious when individuals come into a session and say the results were 'as they expected'; this leads me to explore who did they avoid asking? And, why that might be? You might wish to ask yourself and reflect on your answers to these questions before you engage in a 360.

> **For Reflection**
>
> ▸ What is the very worst thing someone could say in my 360?
>
> ▸ And that is the worst thing because ___

Who annoys you and what don't you like in others?

Several years ago, I was moaning about someone I was working with to a mentor of mine. His response to me was: 'she is just holding up a mirror to the stuff you don't like in yourself.' Boof! What a punch in the stomach that was and whilst my response then was 'don't be ridiculous', I have latterly realized he was right. This is what Carl Jung referred to as 'projective identification' – when we unconsciously project an aspect of ourselves that we dislike, want to get rid of or are ashamed of, onto the other person. This means that we see what we dislike about ourselves in the other person. Therefore, you might think about those who you don't like, who irritate or annoy you and then get specific and reflect on:

- What is it about this other person that I specifically don't like or irritates me?
- What is the quality I am noticing in that other person?
- What does that tell me about me?

> ### For Reflection
>
> Before moving to the next chapter, take a moment to reflect:
>
> - Whose input and feedback will you find of value? Who don't you want to ask?
> - What do you most want to know? What are the questions you will ask? What are the questions you don't want to ask?
> - What are you fearful of? What is at stake for you?

Further Resources

This is a really helpful book to support you in thinking about how you seek, receive and give feedback.

- Stone, D. & Heen, S. (2015). *Thanks for the feedback: The science and art of receiving feedback well.* Penguin.

Chapter 5
Developing self-awareness: the inter-personal component of behaviours

*'Behaviour is what an individual does,
not what they think, feel or believe.'
Emily Dickinson, 1862*

Behaviours are what others see and hear you doing, what you would see and hear on a recording and what the fly on the wall might observe. It is what you say in terms of the words you choose, and subsequently the volume, tone and pace you use to deliver those words. It is also your body language; note that this is not just limited to your facial expressions, it is also how you sit or stand, what movements you use. This is such an important aspect to become aware of, because subtle changes in your facial expression or body stance can completely change how the message is received. I recall receiving some feedback from a manager I was working with who said that my facial expression indicated I had a thought, and that they felt a little judged in that moment. I was, of course, horrified at this feedback, but it was invaluable as I was able to reflect on what might have triggered that behaviour in me and work through it. However, it would be absurd to never show facial expressions or have body language as this would be a barrier to human connection. Therefore, I am not advocating in this Chapter to stop these things; instead, I am proposing that you become more aware of them in order to support and enhance how you show up as a leader. As Amy Cuddy (2015) highlights, your body language shapes who you are.

Getting to grips with this component can be a real challenge – when did you last look at yourself in a mirror as you went through what you would say to your team? When did you last watch a recording of yourself in a team meeting or giving a presentation? If you are anything like me, you will find watching recordings a rather painful experience. I remember during my initial officer training at BRNC Dartmouth, I was recorded delivering a presentation and I was horrified about how I sounded – I had had a completely different perception of self, but I also was able to observe my body language which was probably not a positive experience for the audience! I have thought about that recording on several occasions and it really supported my thinking about how I present. More recently, I worked with an actor when I was preparing a keynote address and, through his support, I was able to see how introducing a few purposeful steps in between sentences could change the way the message was being received.

Through my own work with Dr Eunice Aquilina (a somatic expert), I have been thinking about what my shape is and how I occupy (or not) my space. Somatics is about how we shape our body around our internal physical perceptions and history. When I say shape, I am not talking about being tall, short, thin or fat, I am talking about how well someone takes up their own space, how grounded they are, and whether they are expansive and stepping into their dignity? Often, I see leaders with what I call an 'up and out energy' (like a meerkat), where their feet are not balanced or grounded and they lean forward with a fast pace, high volume delivery. Or we see leaders knocked off course who are shrinking away and trying to make themselves look small; we often see this displayed in groups and teams when individuals don't want to be drawn into a conversation or asked a question.

> **Case Study**
>
> A leader I was working with wanted to have greater impact in team meetings, and we focused on how she might own her dignity and feel her wealth of experience and many successes. Then I was able to give her some feedback on how she was showing up with me with regard to 'how she was occupying her space'. This resulted in her changing her body by having both feet on the floor, feeling the back of the chair on her back and growing a little longer in her spine. The outcome was that she had greater impact when she was speaking in team meetings as she was doing so from a position of being grounded and owning her dignity. I share this anecdote to illustrate the power of your bodies and the impact you, as leaders, can have when you tune into this. This of course is also linked to the intra-personal component of physiological responses.

In addition to gaining awareness of your behaviours it is also important to understand how the environment and system around you impacts how you show up, and how this might influence the behaviours you are using. Systemic thinking highlights that behaviours can only change or adapt as much as the system will allow. Therefore, if you are working on changing behaviours you are likely to find that the system (environment, organizational culture and people) will support and/or inhibit this behavourial change. With this in mind, it is helpful to start reflecting on what might cause you to show up differently with different people and in different contexts.

As highlighted in Chapter 3, all the components are linked together and do not stand alone. Therefore, once you have identified and become aware of how you are behaving, you then need to turn your awareness to develop an understanding of why you are behaving in that way, and what triggered the behaviour. This can often be linked to the intra-personal components, which will be covered in Part 3.

Methods for developing this component

Below are a variety of methods in support of developing this aspect.

Mirrors!

Think about using a mirror when you are going through what you are going to say or present – it is a quick, simple and cheap method. You can also do this through Teams or Zoom. I always encourage the leaders I work with to practise the first three to five sentences of what they are going to say during an address or at the start of a challenging conversation, either in front of a mirror or with me in order to notice the facial expressions they are using and any other body language. This can be a powerful intervention seeing what others will be seeing.

Start noticing

I have a horrible habit of pointing my finger when I am making a point, and it can be perceived as 'finger pointing' or 'directing my point at a particular individual'. Luckily my lovely family shone a light on this and they continue to remind me, but until they pointed it out I was unaware I was doing it, although interestingly my mum does it all the time – an example of how our history shapes us. Therefore, ask those closest to you – what is the thing I do that either irritates you the most/or that you notice? Secondly, start taking momentary pauses at work and just notice what you are doing with your body – are there any trends or habits?

Work with a coach

Case Study

I was working with a team and, as part of the initial diagnostic phase, I spent some time watching them in a team meeting with a focus on the team leader. I noticed how they sat, who looked at who, who fidgeted, etc. More importantly, I recorded who said what, how they said it, and who responded and how. This gave me rich data as to who initiated conversation, who opposed it, who agreed with it. I was then able to sit down with the leader and review his behaviours in the team meeting. This enabled the leader to reflect on how he was showing up in this space and what he might change in order to have more effective team meetings and build greater team participation.

Working with a coach in a one-to-one set-up can also provide the opportunity to focus on behaviours; you can ask your coach to feedback what they are noticing when they are working with you. I often notice how a leader's facial expressions and body language change as they talk about different leadership challenges and/or people in their organization. A coach is particularly helpful in this regard as they can confront what might be uncomfortable, and feedback observations that others often can't – as Blakey and Day (2012) say, move into the 'zone of uncomfortable debate'.

Recording

Whilst many of the coaches I work with have experience of recording themselves and watching it back, many leaders do not, and this is probably due to time and effort. However, recording oneself during a virtual meeting is very simple through platforms such as Zoom or Teams. I acknowledge that behaviours can be different in a virtual environment, and this is itself worthy of reflection. As highlighted by my BRNC story, you may be surprised about what you see. I, therefore, encourage you, where possible, to be recorded in a team meeting and/or giving an address or presentation. Yes, it's hard but in my experience, it reaps dividends.

Watch yourself back and notice:

- What shocks you?
- What would you like to do differently?
- What changes in a virtual environment?

Notice if, when you watch the recording, you start conjuring up a narrative of justification – a sign of potential storytelling and self-deception. Recording is one of the most effective ways of confronting our visible and audible behaviours, because by sitting and watching a recording we must sit with the discomfort of who we are and what we are projecting. The fact that I can remember my Dartmouth recording from 1990 shows the powerful nature of such an intervention. To make this even more effective it would be useful, after you have watched the recording alone, to review it with a coach who might shine a light on what you are choosing not to notice.

From an ethical perspective, if you do choose to record a team meeting or presentation, be sure to let the audience know you are recording and why you are doing so. I have emphasized my personal experience and the challenges I experienced but equally there will be some of you who may be 'naturals', and you will be delighted with the result you see and hear. Reflect on why that might be so and how you can utilize your natural ability in this area to help those around you and further enhance your self-awareness.

Using a 360 with a behavioural focus

As with others' perceptions, using a 360 can be helpful in this space, enabling managers, peers and team members to provide feedback on your behaviours. However, if you use this methodology, be sure to gather feedback on objective evidence through what is said and seen. The danger is that individuals make an interpretation or evaluation of what they are seeing and hearing and give feedback along of the lines of 'I sensed that was important to you' – this is subjective feedback based on the perceptions of the person giving feedback. More helpful feedback would be: 'when you were talking about the budget for coaching, you pointed your finger at the marketing manager; and I noticed you pointed your finger each time you wanted to make a point.' Finger pointing is very powerful so use it sparingly and judiciously at the right time.

For Reflection

Before moving to the next chapter, take a moment to reflect:

- What behaviours do I know I habitually use?
- How would I describe these?
- What behaviours do I think/know I do that I would rather not?
- What would those closest to me at work and home shine a light on?

Further Resources

In exploring vulnerability and emotions this podcast is a resource you might use.

- The Brene Brown Podcast: https://brenebrown.com/podcasts/

PART 3
SELF-AWARENESS: INTRODUCING THE INTRA-PERSONAL COMPONENTS

> *'Explore thyself. Herein are demanded the eye and the nerve.'*
> Henry David Thoreau

This part of the book shines a light on the intra-personal components of self-awareness. These centre on your own personal awareness of what makes you who you are and what your internal frame of reference is. If you are familiar with the Johari Window tool, which looks at what is known to self and what is known to others, the intra-personal components are those which are known to self and may or may not be known by others. In some ways these components can be easier to gain awareness of because it is all down to the individual (you) and there is no reliance on feedback from others or gathering their perceptions. Of course, it can and will involve some deep and dedicated work to unpick these aspects of self-awareness.

As you look at the intra-personal components, you are very likely to readily identify some key aspects of yourself, and you might be saying, 'I already know that about myself,' which may give you the rationale and belief that you are self-aware. However, what is most needed in this space is the deeper, committed work to really get beneath the surface and this is one of the reasons why many of us are not quite as self-aware as we think we are, because we just don't do this deeper dive.

These components are inextricably linked together and can often give you the knowledge as to why you are behaving in the way you are, but they are below the surface and can take time to discover. I like to think of the intra-personal components being like a tangled ball of wool made up of several different colours; when you pull one strand another comes too. It is like this with these elements of self-awareness; when you start unpicking one you will gain awareness of another. Thus, by exploring motivations for example, you may gain awareness of a belief you previously had not been aware of, or a value might highlight why certain physiological responses were triggered at a specific time.

Whilst you aren't relying on data from others to progress the intra-personal components of self-awareness, do not underestimate the nature of the work to do in this space. Shining a light on some of these aspects can be both painful and uncomfortable as they are frequently linked to your histories. You may well discover things you dislike about yourself that you wish to change; this is natural but avoid the desire to achieve instant transformation! I know I am guilty of being impatient and wanting instant results – I am learning that accepting it will take time, and that with time, change is more likely to occur, as opposed to an ineffective impatient fight to try to make the change happen quickly. Changing values and beliefs, for example, that may have been part of your DNA since childhood, is not going to happen overnight. When this is the case, they will often hook you back into ways of behaving – usually when you least expect it or when stressed. Therefore, do remember what was highlighted in Chapter 3 with regard to being kind to yourself and adopt a mindset of reflexivity and self-compassion, rather than one of rumination and criticism.

If you do wish to change something, think about how best to support that process. Working with a coach or therapist is a useful starting point for change, but ultimately, change is down to you. Often once we are aware of something, we can start to change it if we wish. The purpose of this book is to show how to gain self-awareness of these aspects, not how to change them – there are several other self-help books in that space.

The intra-personal components are:

- ▷ Beliefs and Values – Chapter 6 – this chapter is longer than the others because it provides links to so many of the other components.

- Strengths and Weaknesses – Chapter 7
- Motivations – Chapter 8
- Internal Mental State – Chapter 9
- Physiological Responses – Chapter 10

Chapter 6
Developing self-awareness: the intra-personal component of values and beliefs

'Values and beliefs: the driver for how we show up.'
Author, 2025

I have started with this intra-personal component because when I was doing my research, it was the one component which participants most easily and readily identified as being part of self-awareness. Also, it is such a core aspect of our identity, as it is beliefs and values which influence our behaviours, internal mental state, motivations and physiological responses. Therefore, if I had to say which is the most important intra-personal component I would start here. If you start doing a deep dive into this key ingredient it will likely enable you to pull other strands from the tangled ball of wool. Values and beliefs are often unconscious and have been unconsciously underpinning your way of operating for years, so gaining conscious awareness of them will certainly deepen your self-awareness. Once you are clear on your values, you can then check in and identify if your behaviours are in line with these values, that is, are you living and behaving in a way that is aligned to your values? Being clear on values and then finding a way to live and work in a way that aligns to them can bring inner contentment and peace.

> **Case Study**
>
> A leader I was working with identified that his life was increasingly centred around work. He had become constantly connected to his work and was finding it hard to switch off and achieve balance. He had tried several times to change, usually with a New Year's resolution, but kept relapsing to the behaviours. Unpicking the values and beliefs that were driving his approach and behaviour provided a beneficial starting point for him. Firstly, he identified the unhelpful beliefs that were stopping him making the change and in doing so he was able to pinpoint his values that were at stake. Through some reframing, he was able to start experimenting with some alternative belief patterns. Together we explored what was going on in his wider system, because it is hard to change unless something around you also changes. This led to him identifying 'buddies' to support him – an initial small step was finding a morning running buddy. Over time he started to find and achieve more balance in his life.

Values and beliefs are closely aligned and when you use the NLP neurological levels designed by Robert Dilts, you will observe they are at the same level and close to identity. Figure 4 shows the levels and highlights how one self-awareness component can feed into another. My version of this is based on my model of self-awareness and is shown in Figure 4. I have drawn it like an iceberg to illustrate that values and beliefs are deep beneath the surface, close to our identity and who we are, hence the requirement for a 'deep dive'.

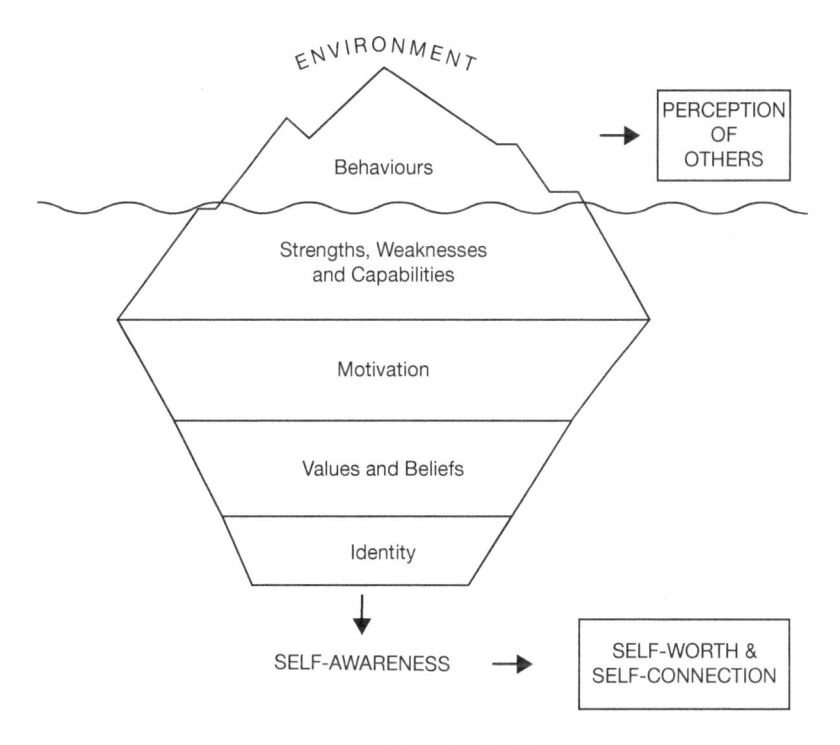

Figure 4: Logical levels of self-awareness

Beliefs

Beliefs are deeply personal, at the very centre of our core, and shape who we are as a person. Often, they have been shaped by our childhood experiences and the family system we have been brought up in. They are usually generalizations that you hold as true; and interestingly, usually without any factual evidence. They will have likely been reinforced and shaped further or may get forgotten due to later life experiences. When you think of beliefs, you might limit your thinking to religious beliefs but be aware there are many more beliefs stemming from your cultural, familial and educational heritage. Furthermore, you might hold some philosophical beliefs. Beliefs can be both helpful and unhelpful – and therefore, can either enable or limit what you do and how you act. To give you an example of a belief, I have become increasingly aware of a family belief I have carried for years which is 'to always put others before yourself and take care of others' which has been reinforced by the family belief system around doing your duty. This means that I often struggle to say 'no' – I push myself hard even when I am not well and I do things I don't always want to do because I feel obliged to. It's interesting that my first career after university was the Royal Navy, in which a fundamental belief stemmed from 'doing my duty' – I was not consciously aware of this belief in 1987 when I applied to join the service, but it is perhaps no surprise I ended up following this path. Beliefs heavily influence the choices you make, but you won't always realize it at the time. Other examples of beliefs are 'it is always important to be on time', or 'I must be the best, otherwise I won't be successful', or 'it is important everyone likes me'. These are just a few examples. Beliefs are important for leaders because they tend to underpin your intentions towards others, so get clear on them.

It is also helpful to identify those beliefs you hold as true, but which are unhelpful and limiting, and work on reframing them to something more supportive of who and how you want to be. For example, in my case, my belief of 'it is always important to put others before myself, and therefore I can't say what I want and need, because if I do, I won't be good enough, and ultimately I won't be loved'. Many psychologists highlight that we have a fundamental human need to be loved and many of our beliefs are underpinned by this need. My belief, which I shared above, has been unhelpful to me because it has prevented me creating space for myself resulting in my becoming over-loaded, tired and even ill because of being rubbish at asking for help and support. I have had to work hard on reframing this belief and believing that 'if I look after myself and am kind to myself, I can actually be even better at serving others'. This is a helpful belief, which also neatly aligns to my value of competence. To this day I am still working on always believing and embodying it because the original belief has been carried through multiple generations of my family on my mother's side. With that in mind, once you have a clearer perspective on your beliefs it might be helpful to think about the following questions.

> **For Reflection**
>
> ▶ How is this belief supporting you? Limiting you?
>
> ▶ How might I reframe this belief to be more liberating and empowering?

Values

Values refer to those things that you attach importance to. They are usually hierarchical, dynamic and abstract concepts which you desire to achieve or be. Values determine your priorities, guide your choices and shape the way you behave towards others. It is values that determine what you perceive to be either right or wrong, and that form your moral compass. Like beliefs, values are often initiated and shaped in your early lives, but the importance or hierarchy you place on them is very likely to change and shift throughout life. Occasionally, usually after a life-changing and significant event or experience, you may have a complete value change – this is when you are likely to hear leaders saying, 'my complete outlook on life has changed.' Like beliefs they can influence your choices.

You will have many values, but there are often a top five or 10 that have the greatest influence on how you judge yourself and make decisions. There are many values and if you do an internet search you will find long lists. Common values are honesty, integrity and family, with other popular ones being authenticity, perfectionism and success. Others you may be less comfortable admitting to are control, status, winning and money. One of my values is competence; closely aligned to a belief that 'if I am competent, I will be successful.' This has driven many choices and behaviours, for example, undertaking and completing a PhD – I desired more recognition of my competence in this field, and if I receive feedback, particularly if it is from someone I don't see as credible, that challenges my competence, I can become defensive and combative. This value also fuels my inner critic.

Values also have a hugely influential impact on your behaviour, particularly when your values are challenged, conflicted or ignored. This can result in conflict behaviours, for example, anger, defensiveness or withdrawal. Whereas when your values are being met and are aligned to what you are doing and where you are working, you are likely to be happier, more content and settled. It is therefore important, if you wish to be at your best, that your work and the organization you work in is broadly aligned to your personal values.

Case Study

The importance of values was evident to me when I was coaching a senior director who came to coaching because he had had some negative 360 feedback. He was not behaving as the organization would wish and through reflecting on his values, he realized that his values were completely out of line with the organization. The easy answer would have been for him to leave, but that was not a desirable or viable option because of other personal factors that were important to him. This led to reflection on what was most important to him, either his values or what was paramount to him at the time, and then as a result a considered rationale as to where he was prepared to compromise. Having gained this awareness, he was able to make a choiceful decision and therefore, he became more content at work, which resulted in his behaviours becoming more aligned to those necessary to work effectively within his organization.

Our values can also conflict with one another, and this can cause negative behaviour.

Case Study

A leader I was working with had a strong value of being independent, not only as a person but the need to be independent financially, which was combined with a belief that it was important to work very hard to be successful. She also wanted to have a family, and family was a core value of hers. When her first baby arrived, she struggled with being the mum she wanted to be, whilst stepping back from work and relying on income from her partner. Her internal narrative started to centre around 'unless I go back to work full time, I am not going to be successful' and 'I will not be financially independent', therefore, 'I am useless and not good enough.' As a result of this, when she returned to work, she was tense and intolerant with her team, snapping at them and generally being unpleasant to work for. Naturally her team were surprised. Through coaching, we were able to unpick why she was behaving in this way and identify the values at stake. This enabled her to identify some interim strategies to manage her values whilst living her life and working in a way that enabled her to spend time with her baby and family.

Methods for developing this component

Below are a variety of methods in support of growing awareness of values and beliefs. I have grouped them up together because they are so closely linked. You can simply start this work by posing yourself the question:

▶ Why do/did I behave in the way I do/did?

And then sit with what emerges and be curious as to what arises. Journalling (see Chapter 3) and drawing may support you in tracking your train of thoughts as you do this work.

Values self-reflection

Just spending time doing some self-reflection around values can be helpful. Here are some questions to kick-start this reflection.

For Reflection

▶ What's important to me?

▶ What has influenced key decisions in my life?

> Think about a time when you felt you have been in a challenging or difficult situation, and ask yourself – what was at stake for me in that scenario?

Alternatively, you can do a values exercise – a couple you might wish to use follow.

Values Exercise

There is no set way of doing this work – you may choose to sit down and focus on it in a disciplined way for a set amount of time. Or you will have it 'at the back of your mind' over days while doing other things. Or you might do it 'all at once'. It is up to you how you approach it. You may like to make notes, draw pictures or mind-maps – this is your choice. How you choose to approach this task might be influenced by your values or beliefs.

Notice if you get caught up in thinking about one area or one value as that might give you some data as to the importance of this value, or it might simply be a distraction. Pay attention to any memories or stories which arise in relation to the value as that can give you an insight into your beliefs.

Looking at the list of values below, notice which ones resonate with you. The list is not exhaustive so feel free to add your own or look at values listed on the internet for inspiration. As you identify ones that resonate with you make a note. Remember these are personal values – about you, not your organization or family. Some of the values on the list below can have multiple meanings, but it is about your meaning and what meaning you make of them.

achievement	friendships
advancement and promotion	growth
adventure	having a family
affection (love and caring)	helping other people
arts	helping society
challenging problems	honesty
change and variety	independence
close relationships	influencing others
community	inner harmony
competence	integrity
cooperation	intellectual status
country	involvement
creativity	job tranquillity
decisiveness	knowledge
democracy	leadership
ecological awareness	location
economic security	loyalty
effectiveness	market position
efficiency	meaningful work
ethical practice	merit
excellence	money
expertise	nature
fame	order (tranquillity, stability, conformity)
fast living	personal development (living up to the fullest use of my potential)
fast-paced work	
financial gain	
freedom	physical challenge

pleasure
power and authority
privacy
public service
purity
quality of what I take part in
quality relationships
recognition (respect from others, status)
religion
reputation
responsibility and accountability
security
self-respect
serenity
sophistication
stability
status
supervising others
time freedom
truth
wealth
wisdom
work under pressure
work with others
working alone

Having potentially identified your values, think about:

- What are your most important values?

- What are your top 10?

- When and why did these values become important to you? (The story may be different for each of your values and may also be related to a belief.)

- How have these values influenced your choices?

As a leader you may also wish to reflect on:

- How do each of these values affect your leadership?

- How do your values shape your leadership style?

In addition – more values work

> **Values Exercise**
>
> You might also reflect on the following, and ask yourself:
>
> ▶ When was I most successful?
>
> ▶ When was I feeling at my happiest and most content (at work and out)?
>
> ▶ When was I feeling most fulfilled?
>
> ▶ When was I most proud of myself?
>
> ▶ When was I dissatisfied (at work and out)?
>
> Having identified those moments, what might that reveal about your values?

Conflict awareness

Some people refer to values as their 'hot buttons', and these are those values that when pushed cause the individual to react in one of the survival modes of flight, fight or freeze. Therefore, another way of identifying values is to think of a time when you have been in conflict with either something or someone and ask yourself:

▶ What was at stake for me?

▶ What was being threatened?

▶ And what was I protecting?

▶ What is important to me?

Here is a personal example. I was doing some leadership development work as an associate consultant with an organization.

I was delivering a workshop when I was told someone, whom I had not met, would be co-facilitating with me. I was angry at this direction and consequently was rather closed with the co-facilitator. When I reflected on what was at stake for me, I realized I had a value around choice – which is one reason I find working for myself so fulfilling in that now I am established, I can choose who I work with, what work I do and when I will work. Therefore, having awareness of our values can be liberating. Identifying values because of conflict often highlights what is important to us.

Values questionnaires and personality measures

There are a variety of questionnaires and personality profiles that look at values and which you can use as a starting point. It may be helpful to combine the outcome from these tools with the values reflection activity above to get a more holistic picture. If you choose to utilize questionnaires or personality profiles, please remember that they are not absolute, conclusive or definitive. They are simply a source of data and another piece of the bigger jigsaw.

Here are a couple of options, which are offered as ideas rather than recommendations:

- The work of Seligman and Peterson has been used to produce the values in action questionnaire, and you can take a free version at: www.viacharacter.org/account/register
- Personality Values Questionnaire developed by Psytech.

Coaching

As with all the components of self-awareness, working with a coach on values can be invaluable.

> **Case Study**
>
> I was working with the owner of a small business who was struggling with work/life balance, who was also in conflict with one of her team and generally not very happy. In our second session, she asked to focus on her personal and company values. She had already come up with some values for her business but was unsure if they were still relevant and valid. She was unsure where to start, but through the coaching process, she identified it would be best to start with personal values. However, she was stuck once again. As she is creative, I used some cards, which had a picture on one side and a value on the other. We started with the pictures, and I asked her to pick out 10 she was most drawn to and then place them in order of preference. We then turned the cards over to reveal the values. This sparked further thoughts and insights and by the end she had identified her top five values.

This shows that sometimes we can start with something more abstract, such as pictures or perhaps poetry to spark awareness. These abstract approaches allow a broader, more encompassing approach rather than requiring a need to be more definitive at the outset of an exercise. With that in mind:

- Notice what and who you are drawn to and perhaps ask yourself, what is it about that/them that appeals to me?

Understanding our history

Freud believed that our past relationships and experiences shaped the way we show up as adults and leaders; in particular the relationships we had with our parents. This means reflecting on our history can be illuminating. This can be done with a coach, therapist, or perhaps a psychoanalyst. The work I have done with my therapist to better understand my family relationships has given me considerable clarity on my belief systems. A coach will be able to support you in identifying and making links to the past, which can provide an understanding, but he or she will not be able to help you face and work through or come to terms with past difficult relationships or trauma. That will require working with an appropriate practitioner. However, by identifying a link to the past, you can then break that link, and by doing so, provide the space for reframing and the creation of new possibilities.

I often ask those I work with about their history so I can have an appreciation of the context I am working with, but also to gain a glimpse of possible beliefs and values.

> ### Case Study
>
> A director I worked with had suffered an abusive and troubled childhood, where he felt out of control and frightened. He also found a love of running so that when his parents were fighting, he would go outside and run. This formed a value around being in control and an underlying belief that you needed to run away from conflict – in work this showed up as him being a micro-manager and whenever there was conflict with his boss, he would withdraw. Through helping him to understand and appreciate where his behaviour stemmed from, he was able to break the link and see that work was not the same environment as that experienced in his early years. This enabled him to find different ways of behaving in the workplace that

> were nicely underpinned by some re-framed beliefs. I advised him that for a longer-term resolution, he perhaps needed to do some work with a therapist to come to terms with and accept his past.

Another source to evoke reflection and insight is the work of Dr Sarah Hill (2023), whose work, *Where Did You Learn to Behave Like That*, identified childhood archetypes. Reading through these archetypes can provide rich data as to possible beliefs. The childhood archetypes are below. As you read through them identify the ones which resonate with you, you may very well find that two or three chime with you.

The childhood archetypes

(included here with the permission of Dr Sarah Hill, Dialogix)

The injured child

Children who have experienced physical, emotional or psychological abuse. There is acute sensitivity to abuses of power, which can result in them putting themselves in harm's way to protect others who they perceive to be vulnerable. They may also strive to occupy positions of power. The childhood voice which lives in the adult: *'Don't hurt me.'*

The star child

Children who have been idolized and go on to idolize others. These children are elevated and celebrated in their family environment, regardless of what they achieve. Their story can lead the adult to connect with a sense of love through idolization. They seek others who can feed this need because it makes them feel worthy, valuable and loved. There can be a desire to seek praise. The childhood voice which lives in the adult: *'Notice me.'*

The compliant child
Children who are made to conform, to follow the rules, to be compliant, to be a 'good girl' or 'good boy'. There is a sense that love is attached to their ability to thrive in a regulated environment which can feel restrictive. This story can lead to a desire to explore and fully understand the rules of each environment. The childhood voice which lives in the adult: *'I can't be what everyone wants me to be all of the time.'*

The carer child
Children who have lost a parent at an early age, or who have been required to look after a parent or who have been required to be constantly happy etc. to support a depressive parent etc. There can be a tendency as an adult to then constantly attend to others' needs at the expense of their own. It can be impossible to put themselves first – they can wear themselves out thinking and worrying about others with little or no regard for their own well-being. The childhood voice which lives in the adult: *'I want to help but I'm trapped and there's no way out of this ___'*

The abandoned child
Children who have experienced abandonment of some kind – physical or emotional – are likely to be left with feelings of 'my parents didn't value me', so why should I value myself? There is an early realization that love is not an everlasting concept. This can lead to difficulties in trusting that enduring relationships are possible – believing instead that repeated abandonment is inevitable. The childhood voice which lives in the adult: *'even the people who love me, leave in the end.'*

The unfairly accused child
Children who have been blamed for things they didn't do or could never have done. There is an imbalance of punishment or the punishment they received outweighed the 'crime'. This can lead to sensitivity about equality, fairness and having a voice. The adult may place a strong emphasis on the importance of enquiry, as a form of compensation for what was not afforded to the child. The childhood voice which lives in the adult: *'Please stop blaming me ___ it's not my fault.'*

The try-harder child
Personified by obedience and dedication to striving for perfection, for success. Failure is not an option. The child's environment is characterized by repeated critique of what he or she achieves. No matter what the child did, it was never good enough. Consequently, they are always striving and driving themselves harder and harder in the pursuit of excellence and perfection. This can continue into adulthood and manifest itself in a fear of failure, a desire to constantly avoid it, and an inability to maintain perspective when failure looms. The adult may be intensely self-critical and intolerant of failure in others. Repeated success at avoiding failure may foster the development of an unrealistic belief in their own invincibility. The childhood voice which lives in the adult: *'I'm doing my best, but I'm scared I'll never be good enough, no matter how hard I try.'*

The compelled child
Children who are strongly driven to realize their potential or a particular goal. They have a weight of expectation placed upon their shoulders from an early age. This includes parents saying things like: 'I want you to have a better life than we do, so please work hard'. It may also be relevant for children who have been burdened to achieve something not yet achieved in

the family, e.g. the first to go to university. It may leave the adult with a particular sensitivity to the idea of letting others down. The childhood voice which lives in the adult: *'I'm worried about letting everyone down __ I'm doing my best not to.'*

The over-protected child
Children who didn't have the opportunity to develop coping mechanisms and a relationship with anxiety, and staying safe, because they were over-protected and often shielded from realities. This can lead to a heightened sense of risk and a belief that they are inadequately prepared to cope with new or changing circumstances. There can also be a sensitivity to abandonment and a desire to keep loved ones safe. The childhood voice which lives in the adult: *'I'm not OK on my own, please don't leave me.'*

The unrecognized child
Children whose parents didn't recognize their different natures. For example, children whose emerging sexuality wasn't recognized or was ignored, or who were different from siblings or parents' expectations. These children may be left with strong feelings of being out of place, acutely aware of not fitting in. As an adult, this may lead them to succumb to pressure to conform or, in contrast, to become rebellious in order to break out of convention. There may be an underlying fear of being an outcast or they may learn to appreciate and celebrate difference. The childhood voice which lives in the adult: *'That's not me. Why won't you see me for who I am?'*

The loved and respected child
Children who are loved and respected regardless of what they did such that they are able to really enjoy life and living. They often feel well-equipped to tackle unfairness, absurdity and

obliviousness through argument and constructive action. This experience can also evoke reactivity that requires attention – not least when they are confronted by a very different reality to their own. The childhood voice which lives in the adult: *'I feel secure in most situations, and I know I'll be alright.'*

(Hill, 2023; pp. 41–45)

> ### For Reflection
>
> Having identified which ones resonate with you, reflect on:
>
> ▶ What is my narrative in relation to this archetype?
>
> ▶ What beliefs am I carrying because of this archetype?

Reflecting on these archetypes can provide a real insight into the beliefs you are carrying which may be either helpful or limiting. For example, if you identify with the 'carer child', you may struggle asking for help or delegating because you have a belief of 'not wanting to burden others'.

> ### For Reflection
>
> Before moving to the next chapter, take a moment to reflect:
>
> ▶ What are your core values and beliefs that shape who you are?
>
> ▶ How do these values and beliefs inform how you lead and behave at work and at home?
>
> ▶ What new awareness have you gained because of spending time exploring this component?

Further Resources

I have included Sarah Hill's book if you want to dive deeper into how your childhood story shapes who you are. The 'Values in Action' questionnaire is free and can provide a starting point to think about values and strengths.

- Hill, S. (2023 – 2nd Edn). *Where did you learn to behave like that?* Dialogix Ltd. UK.

- Strengths Inventory: www.viacharacter.org/account/register

Chapter 7
Developing self-awareness: the intra-personal component of strengths and weaknesses

> *'Everyone, regardless of ability or disability, has strengths and weaknesses, know what yours are.'*
> Brad Cohen,[1] 2008

This is a self-explanatory ingredient in that we all know what strengths and weaknesses are, but, as with all the components, there are layers to explore and discover. As I have previously explained, the components are intertwined. Consequently, our values and beliefs contribute not only to

---

[1] Cohen, B. & Wysocky, L. (2008). *Front of the class: how Tourette Syndrome made me the teacher I never had.* Macmillan.

the strengths we possess but also to our weaknesses. And it is not just what we identify ourselves but what strengths and weaknesses others perceive in us. It may be that we find it easier to identify weaknesses over strengths or vice versa. Furthermore, it may be that having identified one it is highly challenging for us to identify the other. This is worth noticing as it will give you more data, so do please recognize, which one you defer to thinking about first? And do you find it easier to identify your strengths or your weaknesses?

Strengths

Starting with strengths. Personal strengths are the traits, characteristics, capabilities, skills and talents that define who you are. They are often innate in your very being. At times we will limit our strengths to things like kindness, communication skills and being organized. However I encourage you to think more widely about all your skills and capabilities as you might overlook such skills as technical expertise that form part of your strengths profile. You may wish to adopt a positive psychology mindset, where you focus on the strengths and virtues that enable you to thrive. This will mean that you primarily focus on strengths, as there is a school of thought that playing to our strengths is the best way to high performance. There is an adage 'play to your strengths whilst acknowledging your weaknesses'.

Whilst I have just said you may wish to adopt the positive psychology approach and only focus on strengths, it would leave me questioning what you might be avoiding if you ignore the identification of weaknesses. By not looking at weaknesses, you might be stepping into the space of self-delusion and self-deception. A weakness is an ability, skill, or characteristic which is insufficient or does not meet what is either required or needed. Note, it doesn't say what is expected – expectations often arise from your own internal narrative. If you want to be clear on expectations – ask. This may lead you to think that weaknesses are contextual, which is a way you can rationalize them and perhaps use this as an excuse to not tackle them. However, you do have a set of innate characteristics that are both strengths and weaknesses.

Strengths and weaknesses – one and the same?

When we link strengths and weaknesses to the 'others' perceptions' it is important to note that one person's strength might be perceived as a weakness by another. Therefore, this means that a strength if overplayed, used too frequently or in the wrong context can become a weakness. For example:

- Quick to act can become impulsive; dangerous; rash; abrasive.
- Confidence can become arrogance.
- Assertiveness can become overbearing.
- Trusting can become gullible, or a walk-over.
- Helping others can become smothering.
- Collaboration can become indecisive, procrastination.

This is not an exhaustive list, but I encourage you to think about your strengths and what the associated weakness might be. I like to think about this like a volume dial on the speakers – what happens to your strength when you turn the volume up a little or to full volume all the time?

Your shadow side

On the surface, thinking about the strengths and weaknesses component may appear somewhat easier than some of the others, as I am sure you will be able to identify most of your strengths and weaknesses relatively quickly. However, if you wish to go deeper, it might be helpful to start exploring your 'shadow side'. The shadow side of personality is the concept of Carl Jung and is 'composed of all those aspects of ourselves that have a tendency to make us uncomfortable with ourselves' (Hollis, 2007; p. 9). It is the side of our personality which we don't want to be, the feelings and motivations we suppress, the things that we just don't want others to see or that we can't bear to admit to. This is usually at an unconscious level. It's the aspect of ourselves that just doesn't meet our ideals. Bringing a focus onto this aspect can feel somewhat 'dark' and maybe a bit 'unnerving'. However, identifying these aspects of self, then accepting and loving them, is a route to self-connection (the starting point for true connection with others and leading through complexity and uncertainty).

I am not claiming that I have achieved all this work for myself. In, fact I have said that 'I want to kill my shadow side' as I just didn't like the impact on myself, let alone others! However, I have been challenged to start loving this side of myself because killing it would mean losing part of self, and in fact it can't be killed. This concept is important because we all have a shadow side, and our shadow side has grown as a means of protecting and taking care of self – to look after who we are. Moreover, the better we understand our shadow side and come to accept it, the more we can recognize when it comes into play. Without this work it can come alive at moments of stress and high stakes – situations we are in constantly as leaders, whilst leading in this complex and uncertain world.

As doing the work in this space can be unsettling and even scary, it is important to only do it when you have both the capacity and the appropriate support in place. It is also key that in identifying your shadow, you then recognize how it serves you and therefore how it keeps you safe. Having become aware of it, think about what you might do to settle it when it awakens. I have learnt that a silent acknowledgement 'thank you for being here' can help settle mine – but as I have said this is still work in progress! This reinforces the point that this work never stops and is an infinite game.

Methods for developing this component

Here are a few ideas and thoughts you can start using to develop this component. Before you dive into doing any of the activities, consider a few reflective questions you may wish to ask yourself.

For Reflection

- What are my top five strengths?
- What other strengths do I believe I have (remembering strengths are also skills and capabilities as well as characteristics like being organized)?
- What are my weaknesses?
- Which of those weaknesses (overdone strengths) occur most frequently?
- What weaknesses come into play when I am stressed and/or in a high stakes situation?

Having done this, you can see what new data emerges as you do the exercises below. When you disagree with something or simply want to ignore it, be curious and reflect on what that might be about, as this might give you some insight to your shadow side.

Personal performance reports

If you have kept copies of past performance management reports, an accessible and easy starting point is to revisit them and start making a note of strengths and growth areas that were identified by your previous line managers. Do be mindful here that writing a personal performance report is a high-level skill and the quality of the resultant narrative will be dependent on the skill and competence of the reporting manager across so many areas. Thus, I have allowed for perhaps a difference of opinion! Nevertheless, it is always worthwhile to ask yourself is this a fair and balanced picture of me at that specific time? Having made the list spend a moment reflecting.

For Reflection

- Which ones do I agree with?
- Which ones don't I agree with? Why might I disagree with this? (Could this be a shadow side of yourself you are pushing down?)
- Which ones appear frequently that have been identified by different people?
- Do the ones that were identified by others match my own list of strengths and weaknesses?

Strengths finders

There are some excellent free resources available on the internet that can help you think about strengths if you are struggling. There are also others which come with a cost. A popular one is Strengths Scope (www.strengthscope.com/). Alternatively, you can use some prompt cards. I often use some strengths cards when working with my clients as a prompt for thinking about the less obvious strengths. Below is another simple exercise.

The strengths gold mine exercise

Step 1: List 10 Strengths you bring to work (make sure you find 10 – as struggling for the last two or three can help you gain new insight).

Step 2: Highlight one of these strengths.

Name 10 occasions where you utilized this strength.

Step 3: Highlight one of these occasions.

Describe 10 things you did on this occasion.

Personality tests

Personality tests can be supportive frameworks to think about this component, but please remember that they are only a small piece of the jigsaw and are just information. Many of the reports that come with these tests identify strengths and development areas/weaknesses. Some will also identify likely strengths and weaknesses when under stress. The Hogan Development Survey also analyses your potential 'dark' (or shadow) side to gain deeper awareness of this aspect. If you opt for this option, pick a credible test, which has been well researched and work with a coach who can help you unpick the meaning for you.

Childhood story work

The work recommended in Chapter 6 to explore our history, along with the childhood story work, can provide insight into strengths, weaknesses and the shadow side of self, so you may wish to revisit the childhood archetypes with strengths and weaknesses in mind.

Journalling

Journalling (see Chapter 3) is a helpful way of slowing down and can enable you to catch glimpses of your unconscious. With regard to strengths and weaknesses, you might find it helpful to structure your reflective writing around some questions. You could devise your own questions, but here are a couple to get you going.

> ### For Reflection
>
> ▸ What strengths have I used today/this week?
>
> ▸ Who has irritated/annoyed me this week? What was it about that person that irritated/annoyed me? (This is important because often what irritates us about others is often a characteristic within ourselves.)

When coaching leaders, I have challenged them to ask their team members two questions (you must ask both) as follows:

▸ What do I do that you appreciate/value/motivates you (pick one)?

▸ What do I do that irritates you/gets in the way/devalues you?

It is important that if you ask these questions, you make a note of what is being said, you thank the person for their candour and you let them know that you are going to think about their feedback in relation to your leadership. Ensure you avoid responding and reacting, justifying or rationalizing! Of course, you can ask for some examples or more explanation – *but do not* ask 'why' questions! The leaders I have worked with have gained some real insight from doing this, particularly when they have unpacked what was triggered in them and what meaning they are making from the feedback in a coaching session. One leader I worked with took on the challenge of this exercise, but he only asked the first question. He was delighted with what he heard as he gained affirmation and validation but by avoiding the second question, he missed the opportunity to grow his self-awareness. It also revealed his fears about self which he was avoiding looking into – this being his shadow side. The subsequent coaching conversation was able to reveal this to him. You do need to be able to ensure safety for yourself if you ask these questions, so only ask them when you are feeling resourced, resilient and grounded. Avoid asking them if you are stressed or feeling vulnerable. This is a theme that I hope you will be recognizing now that is fundamental in my practice and I cannot emphasize the importance of this approach enough.

Free-fall writing

Alternatively, you might use a 'free-fall' writing technique. To do this effectively:

- ▷ Have a stem sentence, for example, my strengths are ___; or when managing my team I am ___; or I wish I wasn't ___. Create the stem sentence that enables you to develop your awareness of this component.

- ▷ Set a timer and write for that time – two minutes is sufficient.

- Write unedited without letting your pen leave the page – if nothing comes to mind keep writing the stem sentence over and over until something emerges.
- Avoid judging what you write, instead look at it with acceptance.

Learning on the edge

Moments when we are out of our comfort zone and are being tested can often reveal new strengths and weaknesses. Therefore, maybe reflect on previous times when you have been out of your comfort zone and have felt tested. Then reflect on the questions that follow.

> **For Reflection**
> - What enabled you to keep going?
> - What strengths did you draw on during this time?
> - What were you fearful of emerging about yourself?

Sometimes just being in a new group can reveal aspects of our shadow side – my coaching supervisor says that 'groups are transformational and terrifying in equal measure' (Birch, 2021).

I recently attended a webinar about learning on the edge, where a group had participated in a 12-month programme of pushing themselves to the edge to see what was revealed to them. A few thoughts suggested in the webinar and some that I have identified for myself:

- Going on a silent retreat (I understand this is a sure way of having to confront the shadow side).

- Identifying your 'drag'/hidden persona and dressing up as that persona, finding a name for that persona.
- A day of doing absolutely nothing.
- Doing a new hobby/activity.

> **For Reflection**
>
> Before moving to the next Chapter, take a moment to reflect:
>
> - What are your core strengths? And weaknesses?
> - When do you rely on your strengths? Which ones?
> - When are your weaknesses evident? What triggers this?
> - What has emerged about your shadow side?

Further Resources

If you want to find out more about the shadow side, I can recommend:

- This Jungian Life Podcast https://thisjungianlife.com/podcast/
- Barrett, L. (2023). *A Jungian approach to coaching: The theory and practice of turning leaders into people.* Routledge. London, UK.
- Hollis, J. (2008). *Why good people do bad things: Understanding our darker selves.* Penguin.

Chapter 8
Developing self-awareness: the intra-personal component of motivations

> *'What are your unmet needs unconsciously being met through your work and role?'*
> Author, 2025

Fundamentally, our motivations stem from our needs and wants. These needs and wants can be categorized into a hierarchy of needs, as described by Abraham Maslow. There are of course, basic human physiological needs that every human needs to survive, for example, food and water, and then there are the psychological needs to feel good about self, to attain self-esteem and self-actualization. It is these needs I am referring to here, and which underpin your motivations. Motivations are defined as the personal drivers for behaviour. These motivations (psychological needs) are usually derived from your values and beliefs, that is, they arise from what is important to you (see Figure 4 in Chapter 6).

Your motivations will drive how you show up as a leader and shape your leadership approach, so it is critical that you get clear on what they are. For example, if a leader has a value around task accomplishment, they are likely to have a primary focus around a task and its outcomes and, therefore, they may well pay less attention to the individuals and team. They won't be doing this either because they are a bad leader, or because it is wrong, but they will be driven by their need to achieve the task. And, by completing the task, they will feel good about themselves, and their ego will be fuelled and satisfied.

This concept that we do what we do to feel good about ourselves can be a challenging one, because not all the behaviours are acceptable or positive. For example, one person's freedom fighter is another's terrorist. And sometimes motivations can drive negative behaviours. For example, if you have a motivation to impress, and thus a need to get promoted because success is important to you, this could lead to you possibly speaking over others in meetings, becoming dominant and forthright, and then being perceived by others as overbearing.

As highlighted in a previous chapter, I hold a belief that it is important to do 'your duty' and put others before yourself. This belief has led to a need to 'keep quiet and carry on (regardless of how I am feeling and what I want).' The impact of this is that I find it challenging to say what I want and need in any given moment. Part of the drive for writing this book is about me having a voice and saying what I want and therefore, with some irony having stated my previous comment, I am meeting an unmet need in writing – we are all human. And of course, having a published book will fuel my value of competence and ultimately my self-worth.

All of you will have unmet needs, which will emerge unconsciously within your leadership or coaching approach, and work is a way of meeting those needs. This is because you will resolve and meet your need by doing it to/for others; and the manifestation will be an unconscious projection of your need onto another. For example, a leader might need help and support, and this need then leads to them helping and supporting others with perhaps an 'open door policy'. This is a common mantra I hear from overwhelmed leaders and by working with them to understand their needs and unmet needs, they can find a way of changing their behaviours.

> **For Reflection**
>
> ▶ What personal needs are you meeting through your leadership?
>
> ▶ How does being a leader meet these needs?
>
> ▶ What needs are unmet through being a leader and how might you meet these elsewhere?

Thinking about unmet needs is challenging, particularly if we are successful and doing well. They often stem from our childhood stories (see Chapter 6), because, as Dr Sarah Hill says, 'we all have a story of imperfect love'. It took me some time to acknowledge that I have unmet needs, but they are there and now I understand them, I can manage them, so they do not play out unhelpfully in practice.

Some of the common needs I see cropping up in leaders that can result in positive and negative behaviours are:

- A need to be right and get it right
- A need for success
- A need to be liked
- A need to be the best.

With that in mind – what needs underpin your leadership style?

Becoming clear on your needs, drivers and motivations is critical work for leaders as they have such a significant influence on behaviours and how a leadership style is projected. It can be deep, often challenging work but know that we all have needs and it is normal to want to feel good about self and have self-worth. Our ego is forever present! Denying we have needs is self-delusional so be honest with yourself and identify yours; you don't have to share them with others. This component can underpin your understanding of why you behave in the way you do.

Methods for developing this component

Below are a variety of methods in support of developing this component.

Relating to values and beliefs

If you have already spent time doing work around your values and beliefs (Chapter 6), revisiting them with the intent of identifying your motivations, drivers and needs can be a good starting point. You can also use the childhood story archetypes and ask yourself – what does that mean I might need?

For Reflection

As you revisit and reflect on your values and beliefs ask yourself:

- As a result of this value (identify a specific one) what am I motivated to do?
- As a result of this belief, what need do I have?
- If *(insert value)* is important to me, what do I need to do to meet this?
- What is important to me as a leader? And therefore, what am I driven to do/need?

FIRO B

FIRO B is a psychometric that is based on the work of William Schutz which explores an individual's expressed and wanted needs when in a group. It is not a static construct and therefore the results may fluctuate when we are in different contexts. However, the results of the test can be very enlightening. The 'expressed' needs are about how much we express our needs to others and whether we initiate actions because of this need. This means the expressed needs are explicit and can be observed by others. Whereas 'wanted' needs are what we want to be in receipt of from others and are often not expressed. This means that they are often left unsaid but nevertheless drive our behaviour in that group/organization. Schutz identified that we had three fundamental needs when working with others namely, inclusion, control and affection. We need all three of them – the psychometric provides you with an indication as to the extent at that moment in time.

Inclusion: This is about your need to belong, to be with others and how you want to be in groups. Since COVID, I believe that being with others is changing as it is no longer about just being in the presence of others, it is also about the need to be with others physically, in the same space, rather than across a virtual network. There is an increasing need for human connection in the teams and organizations I work in, and this is the result of the dominance and increase in virtual working. 'Wanted Inclusion' relates to the extent to which we expect others to involve and include us in what they are doing. 'Expressed Inclusion' is about how much you initiate interaction with others – for example, how often do you initiate team gatherings and meetings? Some characteristics linked to this need are recognition, validation, attention, participation, involvement and contact.

Control: This relates to your need to influence, lead, take responsibility and make decisions. If you enjoy being a leader, you might expect this to rate highly. It is about how much power you seek. Consequently, if you do have a value around power or status, that might give you some indication as to how this relates to you. However, I know several leaders who are fearful of taking the lead and want to make decisions collaboratively and this might perhaps be driven by a need to be liked. 'Expressed Control' is the degree to which you either take control or lead while 'Wanted Control' is about you wanting others to take the lead and/or assume control. Some characteristics associated with this need are authority, influence, directive and power.

Affection: This need relates to the degree of closeness, connection, sensitivity and openness when relating and working with others. It is about the extent to which we make emotional ties and warm connections with others. 'Expressed Affection' is demonstrated by strong empathy and initiating connection and is often revealed by leaders who are comfortable when expressing their personal feelings and want to be supportive of others. 'Wanted Affection' is about the need for others to be personal with us and encouraging us, driven by a need for others to be warm towards us. Example characteristics of this dimension are sensitive, empathetic, open, affirming, supportive, and warmth. Your results in this dimension can indicate your relationship with being independent and autonomous, and how comfortable or not you are with the loneliness of senior leadership.

> **For Reflection**
>
> To support your thinking about whether your need is expressed or wanted, reflect on:
>
> - How much do you initiate the behaviour (expressed) or rely on others to initiate the behaviour (wanted)?
>
> - To what extent do you want to be in receipt of these behaviours?
>
> - How comfortable are you when others direct their expressed needs towards you (comfortable possibly indicating wanted)?

Completing the test and unpicking what it means for your leadership can provide you with an understanding and appreciation of your drivers.

There are other psychometric tests that look at motivations, which you could also explore, but I believe FIRO B provides invaluable data around our inter-personal needs which are of most relevance from a leadership perspective.

You in conflict/high stakes

We often get into and feel conflict when something is important to us. Therefore, conflict with others and/or organizational principles/strategies and tasks can provide rich data. The challenge is to step back from being in the 'thick of it' and to reflect on what is at stake for you. Below are some reflective questions which can help reveal drivers and motivations.

> **For Reflection**
>
> ▸ What is at stake for me in this situation?
>
> ▸ What is important to me right now?
>
> ▸ What do I need to move forwards?
>
> ▸ What would I say/do if I could say/do anything at all with no consequences?

I use the last question a lot with my clients as it can reveal their own needs and motivations and often make something that seems impossible, possible. It is when we are in conflict that we can really identify what is important to us.

> **For Reflection**
>
> Before moving to the next chapter, take a moment to reflect:
>
> ▸ What are your needs as a leader?

- What drivers and needs underpin your leadership style?
- What unmet personal needs are you meeting through being a leader?

Further Resources

These resources are signposted to support you in thinking about your motivations and needs.

- Frankl, V. E. (1985). *Man's search for meaning*. Simon and Schuster.
- FIRO-B: www.themyersbriggs.com/en-US/Products-and-Services/FIRO

Chapter 9
Developing self-awareness: the intra-personal component of internal mental state

> 'People are not afraid of things, but how they view them.'
> Epictetus, around 55–135 AD

This component refers to both your emotional state (feelings and mood) and cognitive state (thoughts). The linking of emotions and cognitions stems from cognitive behavioural psychology, which seeks to understand the links between thoughts/cognitions, feelings and behaviours. Drawing on NLP, I often say, 'perception is projection', which can be defined as what you are thinking and feeling is then projected through your behaviours as a leader; and therefore, this component is about being clear on your perceptions and thoughts. Your internal state is ever-changing and is triggered in response to what is going on around you in terms of the situation and the people you are with. I am sure you can think of a time when you hear the voice of a certain person or see them coming to speak to you and a whole train of thoughts and feelings are unleashed. This is very much about 'in the moment self-awareness' of what is coming up for you. As with other components, there are interdependencies and in particular, with internal mental state, there is a direct link to the inter-personal component of behaviours. This is because how you are thinking and feeling will directly impact your responses, and therefore behaviours. We usually do this automatically and unconsciously. But imagine if you could break this down and start to have greater influence over your behaviours which others see? By developing your self-awareness in this aspect, you will have much greater understanding and awareness of self and thereby be in a position to start to change the output, that is your behaviours. As Viktor Frankl said: 'between stimulus and response there is a space. In that space is our power to choose our response. In our response lies our growth and our freedom.' Therefore, this ingredient is about you getting clear on the thoughts and feelings that lead to your response so you can start to have more choice.

Emotions/feelings

Turning to emotions and feelings. Firstly, they are one and the same, in that emotions are a strong feeling deriving from your situation, the context you are in and your mood at the time, as well as who is around you. This means that there are occasions when your internal mental state, that is how you are feeling, is being generated by you, and may be governed by how you got out of bed that morning and how you are doing in life.

Start by paying attention to how you are feeling and start naming that feeling. To manage expectations, it is unrealistic to be happy and jolly every single moment of each day of every week, so do continue to identify your feelings including on those days when you are not so positive. If you struggle to name your feelings, Brene Brown's *Atlas of the Heart* (Brown, 2021) is helpful in expanding emotional vocabulary. Alternatively, you can perhaps draw what is emerging for you or reflect and identify an image or metaphor or colour that comes to mind, which you can then use to describe your emotions and feelings.

I frequently talk to my clients about 'triggers', and ask them to consider what is the stimulus for their thoughts and feelings? Or what is it that led you to feel/think that way? By working on this ingredient of self-awareness, where you start to gain a deeper understanding of your thoughts and feelings, you will also likely be able to start to identify the situations and people that trigger you, in Frankl's words the 'stimulus'.

I often find leaders are far more adept at exploring their thoughts and like to analyse and rationalize rather than think about their feelings. This is not surprising as many organizations give supremacy to thinking over feeling. However, to be self-aware, we must give equal weight to both. If you notice yourself finding it easier to identify or describe one over the other, for example thoughts more so than feelings, then ensure you tackle your least preferred one first.

Where to start?

The key to getting to grips with this is to slow everything down and, drawing on Viktor Frankl's quote, start to notice the stimulus and your response. It is best to start this exercise with a particular person or situation in mind. The more times you do this, in as many varied situations as possible, the better.

Step 1: Identify when there is a stimulus or trigger

This is something that sparks your feelings and thoughts. You will most likely be aware of the reaction and response first, unless the emotion is a strong one such as fear, anger, shame or sadness. In the slowing down, go back and identify what was it that triggered this? Was it a certain person, the words they used, a particular situation? The more specific you can be, the better. What was it that you saw or heard that was the trigger?

At this stage be aware of saying to yourself something like 'so and so made me angry; or, that scenario made me lose my confidence'. By thinking and saying this, you are blaming someone or something else for your thoughts, feelings and ultimately your responses. No one can make you happy, sad and angry – as it is you who have chosen this, but we do it unconsciously and automatically, and thus we aren't aware of it. Remember we have freedom to choose. Viktor Frankl was a wise man on this front because he also said, 'Everything can be taken from a man but one thing; the last of the human freedoms – to choose one's attitude in any given set of circumstances, to choose one's own way' (Frankl, 1985; p. 75).

Step 2: Pause

Then *pause* – this will always be a challenge because we often feel we have no time to think in these moments, but this is the space which is highlighted above. You can do this simply by taking a deeper breath and paying attention to your feet on the floor – this will give you the space.

Step 3: Identify what feelings and thoughts are present

Then in the pause you can *identify what feelings and thoughts are present* – this can be done retrospectively, especially when working with a coach or by visualizing yourself back in that moment. Do check in and challenge yourself to ensure you are naming and describing *all* your emotions and doing so accurately.

Step 4: Self-questioning

Ask yourself then – how did those thoughts and feelings influence your behaviour and responses? Once you start to gain awareness, you can then start to make change, but remember, awareness must come first.

Step 5: Optional – taking it deeper

If you want to, go a step deeper – if you wish to deepen this awareness you can link back to values and beliefs by exploring 'how might your values and beliefs have shaped these thoughts and feelings?'

> **Case Study**
>
> I was working with a business owner of an SME with a small team of people. The owner was becoming increasingly stressed and overwhelmed, and she was irritated and annoyed with some of her team. This was resulting in unproductive team meetings and one-to-one interactions. Through the coaching work, we identified her values and beliefs, then what was triggering the sense of overwhelm and annoyance, and what her feelings and thoughts were. At the heart of her responses were her belief 'to please others' and her value around 'having fun'. This led to her taking on more and more, not being able to hold boundaries and then becoming annoyed when her team came to her. I share this story because I am highlighting that the responses we make are often based on messy, irrational and inter-related aspects of our self-awareness.

When I am doing my own work, I am always amazed how my brain has linked things together in what appears to be a highly irrational manner! I work through this with a thinking partner or coach and once I have identified the irrationality, I can make a decision and start to put in place some new thinking patterns or strategies.

This means that stage one is firstly to just start noticing when you are triggered. If you can capture this, you can then identify whether there is a trend in terms of what the stimuli are and in the patterns of how you are likely to respond. Those times we have the strongest reaction will usually be linked to a value and belief. To unlock some thinking on this, I often ask when there has been a strong reaction, 'what is at stake for you? Or what is important to you?'

I was working with a leader around confidence. This leader acknowledged that they could be and needed to be more confident and assertive. We explored if this was always the case or just in particular situations. We identified that it was not true all the time. Instead, it was only evident in certain meetings. Through visualization and recalling one of these meetings, this leader identified that the stimulus was the presence of a particular colleague. We then went on to unpick what feelings were aroused and what thoughts were triggered. Moving on from this, we thought about the times when they had felt confident and were able to be assertive and identified the feelings and thoughts present. This analysis enabled my client to start focusing on these confident thoughts and feelings when she was being triggered by her colleague. It is important to do this sort of work when you are 'in flow' and performing at your best as well as when you are being challenged or are uncomfortable.

By identifying thoughts and feelings when you are: a) triggered or challenged and b) on top of your game, you can then start to choose how to respond in the 'space between stimulus and response'.

Other methods for developing this component

Below are some other ways of developing this component. Working with a coach and a therapist has been the thing that has helped me the most in this component, particularly when they keep me in the space of feelings, so I don't avoid confronting these by reverting to thinking and cognitive analysis!

Feelings, mood and thoughts journal

Start by just noting down unfiltered and unedited thoughts and feelings at different times in the day using these prompts.

In the morning:

- I am feeling ___
- Today is ___

Later in the day:

- I am thinking ___
- I am feeling ___

Note any significant events, meetings etc.
Then you can start to notice if there are any trends and themes. Just doing this for a week will reveal some new insights.

Increasing your emotional literacy

Simply start to notice feelings in songs, poems and books. Or when you are listening to a piece of music or reading, just pause and ask yourself 'how am I feeling?' Avoid the temptation to analyse – just notice.

Thinking pairs

Find yourself a 'Thinking Partner', a person who ideally is trained in the 'Thinking Environment' (Kline, 2009) and dedicate time to work on thoughts and feelings. I meet my 'Thinking Partner' for an hour each month and we each have 30 minutes of allocated time. It is often the second question that evokes more awareness and is often countenanced, 'what more are you thinking, feeling or want to say?' I have also worked with a 'Thinking Partner' where we do 10 minutes once a week. If you are interested in this approach, do read Nancy's books (Kline 2009, 2020).

CBT/CBC and thinking traps

Working with a Cognitive Behavioural Specialist can also support your work in this space. In addition, or alternatively, you can simply start tracking your thoughts and noticing when you fall into one of the thinking traps outlined in the introduction to Part 2 on pages 49–50.

> **Case Study**
>
> I was once working with a leader who was struggling to delegate effectively. I started the work by asking him to identify all the thoughts and feelings that arose when he thought about delegating different tasks to various members of his team. We then homed in on the occasions (in terms of who and what) when he found it the hardest to delegate. I then showed him the list of thinking traps and simply asked, 'which of these might

you fall into?' He looked at me and, in a rather horrified way, said, 'all of them', and 'in fact I don't just do it when delegating I do it all the time'. This awareness gave him the insight to start making changes, re-evaluating some core beliefs and challenging his thinking. Remembering the starting point for change (if wanted) is awareness.

To finish

It is helpful to remember that we are in control of our thoughts and feelings, and we have choice as to what to feel and think in any given moment. The challenge is doing this in the 'heat of the moment'. I like to use the analogy of a control room in which there are several buttons or dials or levers for our feelings and emotions, and sometimes we leave the control room door wide open for anybody, at any time to slip in and just press our buttons. Therefore, what do you need to do to manage when and who opens up that control room – you are in control.

For Reflection

Before moving to the next Chapter, take a moment to reflect:

- What thoughts inhibit me from showing up at my best?
- What one thought can I hold onto, that I believe to be true, which will enable me to be at my best? (Aim to encapsulate this in as few words as possible.)

Further Resources

Here are some introductory resources to support you in thinking about your thought processes. The Steve Peters Ted Talk is a short introduction. If you are new to mindfulness and want to read more about it Chaskalson's book is a helpful starting point.

- Peters, S. (2013). *The chimp paradox: The mind management program to help you achieve success, confidence, and happiness*. TarcherPerigee.

- Steve Peters Ted Talk: www.youtube.com/watch?v=R-KI1D5NPJs

- Chaskalson, M. (2014). *Mindfulness in eight weeks: The revolutionary 8-week plan to clear your mind and calm your life*. HarperCollins UK.

Chapter 10
Developing self-awareness: the intra-personal component of physiological responses

> 'The human body is not an instrument to be used but a realm of one's being to be experienced and explored.'
> Thomas Hanna,[2] 1988

The final intra-personal component is that of physiological responses. This is one that is frequently ignored and forgotten; it was also the element that was mentioned least by

---

[2] Hanna, T. (1988). *Somatics: Reawakening the mind's control of movement, flexibility and health*. Da Capo Life Long/Harper Collins.

my research participants. However, developing awareness of how your body is responding in the moment can provide greater insight into how you are showing up to your team, how you are behaving and the things that trigger you. By physiological responses I mean the reactions in your body such as:

▶ Fluttering heart, a racing heart

▶ How you are breathing – shallow or deep; fast or slow

▶ Temperature – is it the same across the whole body? How does the temperature change or not, in various parts of the body?

▶ Sensations in the body – itches, tweaks, twitches, fidgets, pain, aching.

These responses will be changing and occurring all the time, but due to the cognitive world in which we lead, we are often likely to be disconnected from them. Yet, without awareness of what is going on in your body, how can you be completely self-aware? In my coaching work I often ask, 'where in your body do you notice/feel that?' I am often met with a blank face or a response of either 'I've no idea', or 'I've not thought about that'. This underlines the fact that 'we are not as self-aware as we think we are!'

This is also known as 'interoception', which is about the ability to perceive and understand internal physiological reactions, including heart rate and the activity of the nervous system associated with emotions and feelings. Often these internal sensations are occurring unconsciously, and this is about you bringing them into your awareness (Barrett et al, 2004; Cameron, 2001).

This is linked closely to somatic awareness, where somatics is defined as a 'field within *bodywork* and *movement studies* which emphasizes *internal physical perception* and experience'

(Wikipedia, 2025).[3] Getting connected with the body and how it is reacting, will provide a deeper sense of connection and a more complete picture of our self-awareness.

The work of somatics also prompts you to reflect on how you are showing up in terms of your physical shape. Are you presenting to others from a grounded, centred place where you are occupying your space in terms of your full height, width and depth? I always look at how leaders arrive in my coaching space in terms of the 'shape' they arrive with, e.g.

- Are they hunched over in some way? Head down, shoulders rolled. Or are they standing in their dignity by occupying their full height?

- Are they closed in like a shut book and wanting to look inwards? Rather than unfurled like an open book and ready for connection with others?

- Are they tipping forwards on the balls of their feet? Or tipping backwards onto their heels?

- Where is their energy?

Their shape will give me some clues as to what is going on in their body; more often than not, they are completely unaware of this when they come into the session. This is because we live too much 'on screen' and 'in our heads'! Therefore, with this Chapter, I invite you to get out of your head and start becoming aware of your physiology and what is going on in your body. You can start right now and notice:

- Where is your breathing? (high up in your chest or deeper down to your abdomen)

- How fast or slow is your breathing?

[3] Retrieved from Wikipedia 16 January 2025: https://en.wikipedia.org/wiki/Somatics

I suspect that as you do this simple noticing task, your thoughts will have been interrupted, and something has changed in the moment. This means that when you use your body and notice physiological reactions, you can interrupt patterns of behaviour, thoughts or feelings and thereby perhaps get a different reaction from others or change the outcome. Just as highlighted by Winnie-the-Pooh (Milne, 1926; Chapter 1): 'Here is Edward Bear, coming downstairs now, bump, bump, bump, on the back of his head, behind Christopher Robin. It is, as far as he knows, the only way of coming downstairs, but sometimes he feels that there really is another way, if only he could stop bumping for a moment and think of it (feel it).' I've added in the 'feel it' – paying attention to the physiological responses can stop the bumping.

Methods for developing this component

Yoga and/or Pilates

An obvious starting point is to practise yoga or pilates as a means of starting to pay attention to what is going on within your body. Yoga and pilates classes usually start with some form of breathwork and that discipline is a quick method of building awareness around your breath.

Mindfulness practices

There has been much research highlighting the link between practising mindfulness and developing self-awareness and emotional intelligence. These practices can feel out of our grasp because we are frequently told we must practise them every day for six weeks to achieve change and realize all the benefits mindfulness purports to deliver. However, just by starting to do them 'now and again', for as long as you have capacity for, is a great start. Bite-size chunks, done frequently, of between two and five minutes are better than not doing it at all. There are many apps, such as Be Calm, Headspace, Buddhify to name three, that can support you in this space but beware of getting hooked into scrolling through other media if you choose this approach!

There are two mindfulness practices of particular benefit:

- *Breathwork meditation* – where you start paying attention to, noticing and following your breath, without trying to change it. You can pick the amount of time you do this for – perhaps start with three minutes. Your mind will wander back to the tempting cognitive, problem-solving space – that's natural, just notice that and bring your focus back to your breath. My clients find using an app is the best way to start this.
- *A body scan* – this is particularly good for supporting us to connect with our bodies and to pay attention to physical sensations. I recommend you start with a guided body scan from one of the apps or on YouTube to do this.

Embodied reflection

This is the methodology of combining breathwork and journalling together. My colleague, Johan Frederik Banzhaf, did some research in this area and found that when we combine breathwork with journalling, our self-awareness significantly increases. This would entail doing a breathwork exercise such as a mindfulness breathwork meditation, or the yoga three-part breathing and then journalling what comes up for you. It is important to start the journalling by just capturing immediate, random responses, feelings and thoughts without editing or filtering.

A centring practice

This is something I often use with groups as a starting point and have recommended it to clients particularly before public speaking. However, as a daily practice it significantly enhances connection with our bodies. I have included the exercise below by permission of Dr Eunice Aquilina (2016; pp 28–30).

> ### Exercise
>
> Start by standing, and then aligning your head, shoulders, hips, knees and feet so that you are in a straight line. As you straighten, let your body settle, relax and rest into gravity. Relax your eyes, releasing any tension you are holding there. Relax your jaw, moving your bottom jaw from your top jaw.
>
> Let your shoulders drop. If you are carrying lots of tension, take a deep breath in and, as you do so, hunch your shoulders up to your ears and on your out-breath, let your shoulders drop. You can repeat this a few more times if you are tense.
>
> Now let your breath lengthen and drop down so that you are breathing from your belly.
>
> Start to centre around your vertical line so that you can open yourself up to your own dignity. Let yourself grow a little taller, imagining there is a piece of string pulling you upwards, and that there is some space between each of your vertebrae.
>
> Now centre around your width. Balance your weight across both feet and across all four points of your feet. Imagine you are opening and unfurling like a book opening – allowing yourself to connect to others. This

is about us taking up our own space whilst being open and connected to others.

Next centre in depth, front and back. Find your balance so that you are not pitched forward or tipping backwards. Feel your back, the long muscles at your spine, the backs of your legs. Connect to and acknowledge your history, all those who throughout your life have supported you to become the person you are today.

Finally, return to your breath. If it has become faster and shallower take a moment to lengthen it so you are once again breathing from your belly.

Remember, this is not a cognitive exercise it is a felt one, where we pay attention to and notice our bodies.

For Reflection

Before moving to the next chapter, take a moment to reflect:

Challenge yourself daily, by asking 'how am I showing up today?' And notice your breathing and body shape. This is an important aspect of self-awareness because as Amy Cuddy highlights, our body language shapes who we are, and this undoubtedly impacts how others perceive us (Cuddy, 2015).

Over time, if you practise just some or all these practices you will start to become more centred and grounded, which supports the full development of self-connection which I talk about in Chapter 11.

Further Resources

The Ted Talk highlights how our body shape and body language can impact our hormonal chemical balance. The book is a deeper dive into the physiological component of self-awareness.

- ▶ Amy Cuddy Ted Talk: www.youtube.com/watch?v=Ks-_Mh1QhMc

- ▶ Aquilina, E. (2016). *Embodying authenticity: A somatic path to transforming self, team and organisation.* Troubador Publishing Ltd.

PART 4
SELF-CONNECTION THE ROUTE TO LEADING THROUGH UNCERTAINTY: AN INTRODUCTION

> '*You alone are enough.*'
> Maya Angelou

Having started the journey of self-awareness, the next stage is to take it to a deeper level by moving towards self-connection. It is this work, where you can start letting go of your ego, that will help you to start developing 'negative capability', which in turn will enable you to sit in that place of embracing 'uncertainties, mysteries, doubts, without any irritable reaching after fact and reason'. This is what will underpin your leadership when leading in a VUCA world, which you may recall means Volatile, Uncertain, Complex and Ambiguous.

As previously highlighted, the work never stops and is ongoing, but it is all too easy to tip from self-awareness into self-delusion, deception or hubris and therefore I have included a chapter on this.

Whilst the work to develop each of the components may be challenging and difficult, this next step is the most difficult – the step of accepting and loving all parts of self and knowing and believing the self-worth that we have, without being self-delusional or hubristic. It is such a challenge which is why very few leaders and individuals can sustain 'negative capability'.

Chapter 11
Self-connection for great leadership

'The privilege of a lifetime is to become who you truly are.'
Carl Jung

What is self-connection?

As highlighted in Chapter 1, self-connection is all about self-acceptance and becoming comfortable with who you are. This means that you must acknowledge that you are not perfect, you do not have all the answers, you will make mistakes, and that you live with vulnerability. Vulnerability is not weakness, rather it is about showing emotions and admitting and allowing your weaknesses to be known, for example, 'I haven't got all the answers or ideas here.' Brene Brown highlights that it is about your willingness to face risk, uncertainty and/or emotional exposure, and it is in fact a measure of courage (Brown, 2015), not a weakness. Through this acceptance that you are not perfect and have vulnerabilities, you will naturally start to move towards self-connection.

This is like the concept of Eric Berne's (a Canadian-born psychiatrist) ego state adult-adult, 'I'm OK, you're OK' (Stewart and Joines, 2012). Berne's adult ego state is about you operating in the present of the here and now, without your behaviours being unduly and unconsciously impacted unhealthily by the past. You achieve this through self-awareness because you will have done the work on understanding the origins of the intra-personal components which then influence your behaviours (the inter-personal). This is about you taking responsibility for all aspects of self, and allowing your ego to be calm, settled and at peace. Ultimately, self-connection is the belief and embodiment of being good enough and, to pinch a line from a Barry White song, knowing that 'you are okay just the way you are'.

At this point it is important to emphasize that self-connection is not about you not changing, it is about evolving. Taking a concept from Gestalt psychology, change happens when you accept who you are. This means you will be changing and growing within the space of self-connection through the acceptance of self.

Self-connection is important to leaders leading teams through tumultuous times and situations because to get the best from a team, you must build trust, minimize fear and get to know them, i.e. connect with them. As highlighted by Gergen (Gergen, 2009), this connection can only be achieved by connecting with self. Figure 5 summarizes this.

```
         ┌─────────────────┐
         │ Understand what │
         │ self-awareness is│
         └────────┬────────┘
                  │
                  ▼
┌──────────────┐    ┌──────────────┐
│  Work on &   │───▶│  Build self- │
│ develop self-│    │  knowledge   │
│  awareness   │    └──────────────┘
└──────────────┘
        │
        ▼
   ┌──────────────┐
   │ Develop self-│◀──┐
   │  connection  │   │
   └──────┬───────┘   │
          │           │
          ▼           │
   ┌──────────────┐   │
   │Develop deeper│   │
   │connection with├──┘
   │others and team│
   └──────────────┘
```

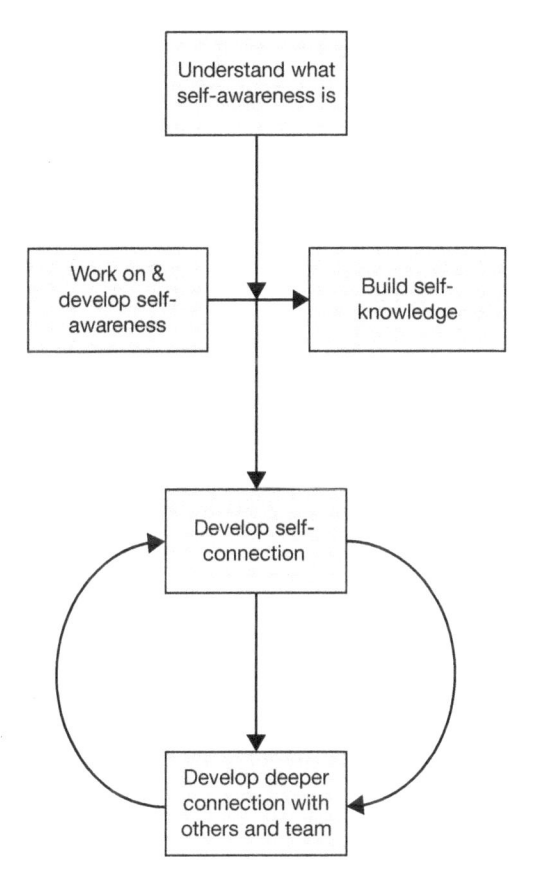

Figure 5: From self-awareness to self-connection and leading others

Why does self-awareness lead to self-connection?

Figure 5 highlights that developing self-awareness leads to self-knowledge and then self-connection. This is because the more work you do on developing self awareness, the deeper you get to know and understand yourself. This is the route to knowing and becoming your authentic self. Any work you do on one or all the components of the construct results in an unpicking and understanding of what makes you who you are. This is because each ingredient can provide a route through to self-connection as follows.

Inter-personal components

If you are open to being vulnerable and not perfect, you can open yourself up to feedback from others about how they are seeing and experiencing you. When you then explore how others might have developed their perceptions, you can start to link this to your own understanding. You can begin to explore why you behaved in a certain way. Which values or beliefs or motivation might have driven your behaviour in that instance?

Values

Getting clear on values and then living by values can provide a sense of inner peace, which undoubtedly supports self-acceptance and connection. The challenge is when the system around you either inhibits or prevents you living and working according to your values. However, awareness of this can support you in finding peace.

Beliefs

Becoming clear on your beliefs and what shaped them can support the process of accepting self and enabling greater choice in terms of how helpful or unhelpful that belief is to the way you want to be. The key question here is 'do you want it?' For example, you might have a belief around 'I have to be strong, and I can't ask for help' – start by asking yourself how that belief is serving you? How was that belief shaped? What does it mean for you today? You then start to have choice about whether you wish to continue to live and lead according to this belief or whether it might be helpful to change it.

Strengths and weaknesses

Depending on whether you choose to analyse strengths or weaknesses first, doing some work to get clear on the opposite one will support work in self-compassion and accepting all of self. We all have strengths and weaknesses and often they have been developed as a means of keeping us safe, enabling us to fit in and belong – it is okay to have both. It is acceptable to prefer thinking about one more than the other – that is all normal. The challenge is to identify both.

Motivations

In terms of accepting self, this is about recognizing that we all have personal needs (often linked to a value) and that those needs must be met. Noting that after the basic physiological needs, we all have needs for love, belonging and safety. It is worth identifying if and where those needs of love, belonging and safety are being met. Often, we can seek to meet those needs through our work, albeit unconsciously.

Internal mental state

Getting clear on how your thoughts and feelings link to other components and behaviours is supportive. Once you start to take responsibility for this, you are moving closer to self-acceptance.

Physiological responses

This is about you connecting with your body and not just living in your head. This is key to self-connection – you can't just connect with your mental cognitive elements!

Figure 5 makes the step from self-awareness to self-connection appear to be a natural flow. However, it is not that simple because, once you know and understand yourself, the challenge then is to accept and love yourself (even the uglies – the bits you don't like, that you might have pushed away and forgotten)! This is not easy work.

> ### For Reflection
>
> To start with perhaps take a temperature check and reflect on:
>
> ▶ On a scale of 1–10, how comfortable do I feel in my own skin?
>
> ▶ How at peace with self am I?
>
> ▶ How compassionate to myself am I?

Watch out!

Self-acceptance is not a justification to behave in unacceptable ways and run rough-shod over others by saying 'it's all about me loving myself'! I have a personality type (made-up) known as 'FIG JAM', which stands for 'F___K I'm Good, Just Ask Me'! I am sure you will know leaders like this where their egos are out there, they are self-publicists with their eyes on the prize (whatever that is), but they are in no way connected to others on any meaningful level. These leaders love themselves for sure, but that is not self-connection because they have not acknowledged that they have vulnerabilities, weaknesses and imperfections. Rather self-connection is about holding one's ego in balance and accepting others through accepting self. It is also about changing and evolving because the more self-aware we become, the more we evolve and develop. That is why in Figure 5 there are arrows going from self-connection to connection to others, and back again. This is the dynamic nature of self-awareness and self-connection in that every time you are in the presence of others and lead them through something, you will be able to gain more awareness of self, and it is this connection with others that provides additional opportunities for more work on self and self-connection.

How to get there?

Working through to self-acceptance is not easy and can be tough. Part of self-acceptance is about being kind and compassionate to yourself and, with that in mind, it is important to avoid seeking instant gratification and results and to accept that this can and probably will take time. Also, there will be times when we can fully connect to self, know that we are OK and good enough and other times/scenarios that take us off track. This may manifest in you being fully connected to self when with your team at work, but out of work (perhaps with parents), you might feel inadequate, not good enough and full of self-flagellation. As evidenced by the Carl Jung quote at the start of this Chapter – this is a lifetime's work. This means that our work on self is never done.

I will discuss below what is needed to maintain self-connection and what the barriers are. Firstly, some thoughts on how to move towards self-compassion and self-acceptance.

Personal care and finding space

Taking time to look after yourself and do what you want, and need, is a good start in this space. It is easy to put work and others before self and join what I term 'the self-sacrificing club'. Lots of leaders I work with talk about the needs of work; they work long hours, have poor work-life balance, perhaps sacrifice family life and are constantly on work business. If this is the case and you are not looking after yourself, how can you possibly look after your team and your business/organization?

With that in mind, find moments (I mean moments, even just five minutes) when you can do something to take care of yourself in the way you want to, perhaps listening to music, grabbing some fresh air, eating something healthy or the like. Small moments are a good way to start. Remembering in Tom Hanks' words 'doing the work/the self-care is the win, not the results'.

Love and kindness meditation and/or mindfulness practices

Research has shown that undertaking mindfulness practices, or love and kindness meditations, directly links to self-compassion. As indicated in Chapter 10, there are many apps, and YouTube clips available that can get you started in this space. There was some research that compared the positivity ratios of two groups of students. One group practised a love and kindness meditation for five minutes every day and the other group just carried on as usual. The positivity of the group undertaking the love and kindness meditation significantly increased (Fredrickson, 2011).

Body work

Anything that helps us connect to our bodies can support us in developing self-acceptance and can also underpin personal care and finding space. Body work means doing something like yoga, pilates, tai chi, or general exercise. Research has shown that yoga can lead to a significant increase in self-acceptance (Casey et al, 2018). What is important is to find something you can fit into your busy life and sustain. I was once working with a leader who introduced tai chi once a week into the business and offered it to anyone who wished to take part. Whilst I am sure he was doing this to meet a personal need, I am in no doubt that it benefitted the team and enhanced the relationships and feelings at work. These practices also emphasize that it is the journey and acceptance of limitations rather than being perfect that matters.

If you are feeling that you lack confidence, which is hampering self-acceptance, the work of Amy Cuddy (2015) will be of benefit. This involves the use of short power (two minutes) poses to change the chemical hormonal balance in your body. This process can help reduce the levels of stress hormones (adrenaline and cortisol) in your body and increase levels of testosterone which can underpin confidence and grounding. I have used this myself and signposted several individuals and teams to Amy's work. Some yoga poses also work well in this space.

Challenging negative self-talk

If you are someone who has a persistent and loud inner critic, doing work to challenge and re-programme negative self-talk with a coach or therapist will support self-acceptance. Cognitive behavioural therapy and coaching is a good approach in this space.

Alternatively, using an incisive question (taken from Nancy Kline's work), which we can keep returning to, to challenge a limiting belief can also be a valuable starting point. For example, 'if I knew I was good enough just the way I am, how would I feel now/in this meeting?' or, 'if I knew I was enough, what would I think now?' Notice the present tense of now – this is important because it will take your mind to the here and now, and the adult ego state highlighted above. With some clients I have found just referring to the question can bring about a shift towards inner peace. If you can identify a supporting incisive question, think about writing it down so you can look at it when you need to.

Daily mantras

> **Case Study**
>
> A leader I was working with came to a reflection, towards the end of the session, of 'I am doing my best'. As she stated this, I noticed a shift in her physiology in that her eyes softened, she sat more upright and it felt lighter, as some tension seemed to slip away. I asked her how it might be to say I am doing my best to herself, while looking in the mirror morning and night and notice if anything shifted or changed. She came into a later session and reported that she was feeling more at ease with the pace and pressure of work, because she was starting to embody that she was doing her best.

Daily mantras are one way of finding inner tranquillity (Raval, 2024).

Journalling

Journalling (see Chapter 3) can aid self-appreciation and thereby self-acceptance. It is also okay to capture things you are struggling with or finding challenging as we can't be sailing smoothly all the time. Simple gratitude journalling, e.g. 'today I am grateful for ___' is enough. One leader I was working with was feeling inadequate in a new job role and so she started to capture reflections around:

- One thing I achieved today ___ (this can be something small, such as getting to a meeting on time).

- One thing that made me smile ___ (again, something small, like something you heard on the radio, or seeing a bird in the garden).

- What have I got to look forward to ___ (again, something small as a treat such as watching a film, or having a pizza).

This daily practice started to reinforce that she was enough how she was. There are plenty of tips on the web and apps that can provide other suggestions for journalling. The important thing is to find a methodology that underpins self-compassion and that you like. If using an app and you find yourself 'doom scrolling', maybe resort to an old-fashioned paper and pen!

Parts integration

There are often aspects of our internal self which are in conflict, e.g. a value and a belief, or two values. This can lead to stress, discontentment, being moody, being snappy with others, perhaps shouting at others to name but a few. Remember the leader I talked about in an earlier Chapter who had returned to work after having a baby, and had a value around independence, including being financially independent but also a belief that to be a good parent, she shouldn't be at work all the time. There were two parts to be integrated – the value of independence and being a good mother. There will be parts in you which might conflict with one another and in order to settle and find inner self-connection, they will need to be integrated in some way. One way of tackling these conflicts is to do a 'parts integration' exercise. This is best done with a coach, but through reflection, you could take yourself through the initial steps and start the work.

> **Exercise**
>
> ▸ Identify the two parts that conflict with one another, and acknowledge they are there and part of who you are.
>
> ▸ Think about how each of these parts serve you. What is the positive impact of them?
>
> ▸ What are the emotions associated with each element? We are aiming to integrate both parts into who we are and accept that both can serve us.

Shadow work

As highlighted in earlier Chapters, we all have a shadow side and becoming who we are means identifying this and accepting it. As Carl Jung said; 'until you make the unconscious, conscious, it will direct your life and you will call it fate.'

If you have done the reflection around childhood archetypes in Chapter 6, you will have already started identifying your shadow side. Other ways of identifying shadow side is through journalling where you slow down, get curious and allow yourself to capture whatever emerges (I often ask my clients for their first thought, which is the best thought) – this will often allow glimpses of the unconscious to emerge.

> **For Reflection**
>
> In addition to earlier reflective questions, others which might support this work are:
>
> ▸ What do I dislike/hate about myself?
>
> ▸ What do I feel resentment about?

> - What and who do I envy?
> - What do I find fascinating and inspiring in others?
> - What do I moan/complain about (things and people)?

This is deep work, and I recommend only doing it if you are feeling resourced and have the right support in place.

> ### For Reflection
> - What's the work I need to do?
> - How might I do that work?
> - How will I make time for this?
> - What will I do to keep myself accountable?

What are the barriers to self-connection?

Even when we are motivated and curious to do this deep work, there are still barriers to making the step of self-connection. A few are discussed below.

Past trauma and what's left unhealed

If you have had traumatic events in your life or moments in time when things were left unfinished in terms of healing, you will find it hard to completely connect with self. The sense of being unhealed comes from not only trauma, but also other moments in time. For example, when there has been an unsatisfactory ending, being made redundant, or not being promoted when you had given your all. These sorts of instances can leave a sense of unfinished business, incompleteness and loss which results in feelings of anguish, hopelessness, despair, sadness and grief. All of this, if ignored and 'locked away', will result in you not embracing your whole self, because you can feel powerlessness. Therefore, if this is the case do think about working through this.

Shame

Shame is such a destructive feeling because it focuses on self, rather than what happened. Shame can leave a sense of not feeling okay, and not good. Brene Brown defines shame as 'the intensely painful feeling or experience of believing that we are flawed and therefore unworthy of love, belonging and connection' (Brown, 2021; p. 137). The trouble with feeling shame is that we don't like to talk about it, we are embarrassed about it, and this stops acceptance of self. The antithesis of shame is love and joy, so with that in mind, the love and kindness meditation, daily mantras and similar practices may be good places to start. Brene Brown also highlights that perfectionism is close to shame because 'perfectionism tells us that our mistakes are personal defects' (Brown, 2021; p. 143). This inhibits the development of self-connection and negative capability. Therefore, if you have a value around perfectionism, this will be a challenging space for you to work in because you will not be able to connect with the adult ego state unless you are being and doing perfectly!

Comparison

This is one barrier I am very familiar with. I have lived a life of comparing myself with others, where the driver has said to me not only get to where the others are but be better than them! Hence the PhD journey. The trouble with comparison is that you will never 'be good enough'. To challenge this, ask yourself the following questions:

> **For Reflection**
>
> ▶ What's important to me?
>
> ▶ What do I want?

It's not okay to be feeling down or have a bad day

The British mantras of 'stiff upper lip' and 'keep calm and carry on' inhibit the 'you are ok' perspective, because it infers you can never feel low, have a bad day or be less than positive. It is also clearly not in the self-compassion space. Once we learn that it is okay and natural to not only be down and have an off day, but to also express it, we have started to accept ourselves. By admitting that all is not well, we are in touch with our vulnerability, we are okay with not being perfect and we are more at peace with ourselves.

> **For Reflection**
>
> Before moving on ask yourself:
>
> ▶ What might be getting in the way of me connecting with self?
>
> ▶ What stops me being compassionate and kind to self?

How can self-connection be sustained and what are the derailers?

I have already indicated that self-connection is not a static way of being. If you change jobs, get promoted or retire then you may find yourself having to do some more work in this space. As well as the barriers above, a key derailer to self-connection is low resilience and tiredness. I notice that it is harder to be present with 'I'm okay', when I am tired and low on energy, which is why personal care and finding space are so important. Therefore, it is useful to also become aware of your resilience levels and what you need to do to maintain your resilience. The more self-aware you are, the more likely you are to be resilient; doing the initial and ongoing work on self-awareness is thus pivotal to an ongoing resilience in support of self-acceptance. In thinking about what resilience means to you, one definition is: 'Resilience is about being open to learning and growth, being able to take risks because of a sense of being able to deal with the consequences of that risk. Resilience does not protect us from the setback, but we are able to manage our way through it' (Pemberton, 2015; p. 3).

> **For Reflection**
>
> In thinking about resilience:
>
> ▸ How do you know you are resilient?
> ▸ What do you need to do to maintain resilience?
> ▸ How do you know your resilience is being tested?

Final reflections

To embrace negative capability and lead effectively in a VUCA world, self-connection is the work to be done but you can only do this once you:

a) Know what self-awareness is

b) Get curious and motivated to do the work

c) Start working on self-awareness

d) Acknowledge that this is an infinite game of ongoing work on self – if you were to say to me, 'I don't need this work Julia, I am already self-aware', I would know you are not because you will be promoting ego and have not grasped the dynamic nature of what self-awareness is.

> **For Reflection**
>
> Before moving to the next Chapter, take a moment to reflect:
>
> ▸ What's emerging for you as you think about self-connection?
>
> ▸ What do you need to pay attention to?
>
> ▸ How will you hold yourself accountable to do this work?

Further Resources

Here are some additional resources to support you on the journey of self-acceptance.

- Brown, B. (2022). *The gifts of imperfection: Let go of who you think you're supposed to be and embrace who you are.* Simon and Schuster.

- Cuddy, A. (2015). *Presence: Bringing your boldest self to your biggest challenges.* Hachette, UK.

Chapter 12
Self-awareness or self-delusion

> *'Of all deceivers fear most yourself!'*
> Søren Kierkegaard, 1843

When I was doing my research, I was asked 'is it self-awareness or self-delusion?' A great question, to which I would also add in self-deception and hubris. How can we know if we are self-aware or if we are merely deluding ourselves? It is easy to slip into a delusional space because humans naturally wish to justify their position, thoughts, feelings and actions. This is not wrong; it is just human nature. Your neurology likes to keep you safe and avoid possible threats to ego, so, of course, you will 'story tell'; it's a survival instinct. You may also slip into this tendency to avoid confronting your shadow and the aspects of yourself you don't really like. If you are noticing yourself saying 'I don't do that, I'm not self-deluded', perhaps pause and ask yourself the questions below.

> **For Reflection**
> - What are you protecting here?
> - What are you avoiding tackling or facing?
> - What are you afraid of?

This behaviour is driven by a need to fit in and be seen as good enough, but this is striving to be good enough rather than embodying and believing you are good enough.

The reality is that, until now, you have probably not had any clarity or definition as to what self-awareness is, so the chances are you have been self-delusional in claiming that you are. Secondly, how prepared have you been to do the deep reflective work required to be self-aware?

You should by now appreciate what self-awareness is, but are you clear as to what self-delusion, self-deception and hubris are? Like self-awareness, self-delusion and self-deception are complex constructs with multiple definitions. This is undoubtedly due to the multiple interpretations of what is 'self?' Here are a few perspectives on each:

Self-delusion is the action of deluding oneself; a failure to recognize reality. This is challenging because it depends on your philosophical perspectives of what is reality. For example; claiming that you do not have a shadow side, that you are perfect in all ways, and brilliant. This could be a narcissistic person.

Self-deception is a process of denying or rationalizing away the relevance, significance or importance of opposing evidence. This could easily fall into the 'storytelling' camp, when we justify so that we can ignore something such as feedback, others' perceptions, or our projections onto others. This is evidenced when someone is continually making excuses for self, blaming others, acting and feeling defensive.

Hubris is a personality quality of extreme or excessive pride or dangerous overconfidence, often in combination with arrogance (or complacency!). It is 'an inflated sense of one's own innate abilities' (Brown, 2021; p. 243). Those who believe they are self-aware and make statements such as 'I am very self-aware' are demonstrating hubris. Hubris would be the FIG JAM personality mentioned in Chapter 11, that someone who is craving and seeking self-esteem rather than embodying it through self-awareness and self-connection.

To provide some clarity, Table 1 offers an outline differentiation between self-deception and self-delusion, but both are blockages to self-awareness. Both self-delusion and self-deception can be experienced by someone who thinks they are self-aware.

What causes this?

Self-deception and self-delusion are often due to a lack of self-knowledge and where you engage in 'confirmatory bias,' i.e. seeking out information to confirm your views, thoughts and beliefs. It can also occur when you are wanting to protect yourself and fit in.

It is often a coach who can say something to an individual that others can't because the coaching is objective, and the coaching relationship builds trust and connection, which provides a space for this to be tackled. Several leaders have said to me as their coach: 'thank you for saying to me what others won't or can't.'

Table 1: Self-deception and self-delusion

Self-deception	Self-delusion
▶ Can be conscious or unconscious. ▶ Umbrella term for all biased information processing. ▶ Often serves a purpose e.g. protecting one's ego, avoiding discomfort, or maintaining a positive self-image. ▶ An example may be constantly thinking that you are a brilliant leader and can do everything unaided. ▶ Likely to see denial and rationalization with self-deception.	▶ Often unconscious. ▶ Irrational – beliefs are not based on evidence. ▶ Not recognizing reality. ▶ An unrealistic view of oneself. ▶ A persistent strong view despite contrary evidence e.g. someone claiming they are self-aware when they don't know what it is; believing you are a warm person despite feedback that you are cold, unforgiving and not open.

Case Study

I once worked with a leader whose job role had been changed. He was out of sorts and was in a space of blaming others rather than looking inwards, as he was struggling with the new role and did not want to ask for support. I am sure that he was unconsciously protecting his ego. Therefore, rather than acknowledging he

Self-awareness or self-delusion | 161

> needed support, he continued with a blinkered vision which resulted in his performance deteriorating. This led to him receiving feedback from his line manager, which he denied and blamed his manager for. It took some time for this leader to see the reality of his thinking – he was in the space of self-delusion.

As leaders, this can also be because you surround yourself with 'yes-men/women' who never oppose or challenge you; or as a result of recruiting people to your team that are like you. This results in a successful 'echo chamber' rather than critical thinking.

Self-deception and self-delusion also stem from a lack of humility, because those who demonstrate humility will know that the work never stops, that you can never be the finished product, and the development of self-awareness is an infinite game.

How can you avoid this?

Self-knowledge

By doing deep self-awareness work and developing self-knowledge of your beliefs, biases, assumptions and triggers you will be well on the way to avoiding self-deception and self-delusion. This can be cemented by holding the belief that this is ongoing work and a life's work.

Seeking feedback

Seeking feedback was discussed in Chapter 4. This must include thinking about what are you avoiding and are fearful of asking. Maybe ask yourself the following questions.

> **For Reflection**
> - What do I not want to hear?
> - What am I dreading/fearful of?
> - What am I avoiding?

Humility

If you have already accepted you are not perfect, that you have vulnerabilities, weaknesses and are ever evolving, you will already have found humility. Humility is about us being open to learning and knowing that we are never a complete, finished product. Brene Brown defines humility as, 'openness to new learning combined with a balanced and accurate assessment of our contributions, including our strengths, imperfections, and opportunities for growth' (Brown, 2021; p. 245). This is not about you downplaying your strengths and achievements, rather it is about acknowledging your contributions within the context of what others might have done around you. It is also about us appreciating that we only have *a* perspective or view, rather than *the view/answer* and that the work must be ongoing.

Challenging assumptions

It is natural that you have assumptions – they help you navigate life and the world around you. However, they can be a barrier to self-awareness and connecting with others. If you live your assumptions as true, you are likely to be slipping into some form of self-delusion or self-deception. Here are a few questions to ask yourself when you are working on self-awareness.

> **For Reflection**
>
> ▸ What might you be assuming about _____? Maybe ask this question a few times to identify all your possible assumptions.
>
> ▸ Are any of these true? If you believe they are true – how do you know? What evidence have you got?
>
> ▸ What are you assuming that is stopping you facing/confronting _____?

Confronting what/who you don't like or disagree with

Identifying the things and people you dislike and/or disagree with can be revealing. These people and things are often holding a mirror up to something we don't like about self. By confronting this thought and perspective you can avoid self-deception and self-delusion. When this situation occurs, start reflecting by asking:

▸ What is it about this person or situation that I specifically dislike or find annoying? If that was an aspect of self – how would I feel? Notice your response to this, as that might be a clue as to whether you are in the self-delusional space. If you remain curious, you are more likely to be moving towards self-awareness.

▸ What or who might that person be representing to me?

Other practices

Other practices that have been discussed in earlier Chapters are also helpful here, for example:

- Mindfulness practices (Chapter 10, p. xx)
- Journalling (Chapter 3, p. xx)
- Self-reflection around beliefs (Chapter 6).

> **For Reflection**
>
> Before moving to the next Chapter, take a moment to reflect.
>
> It is easy and understandable that we slip into the space of self-deception and self-delusion as there are many fear-based organizations where we need to protect ourselves to fit in and be successful. However, by acknowledging this we can ensure we move towards self-awareness.
>
> - What might be the hooks and triggers that cause you to slip into self-deception and self-delusion?
> - What will be the signs that you have gone to that place?
> - Who in your network can hold the mirror up to you?

Further Resources

If you want a greater understanding of hubris and self-delusion try these resources:

- Owen, D. (2020). *Hubris: The road to Donald Trump: Power, populism, narcissism.* Methuen.
- Podcast: Hidden Brain (hiddenbrain.org).

Chapter 13
Facilitating self-awareness in others

'You cannot teach a man anything. You can only help him discover it within himself.'
Galileo Galilei

As a leader you will be responsible for guiding and developing your team, and you might now be thinking 'if I am doing all this work to develop my self-awareness, why don't I do that for my team?' Or you might be guilty of skipping on past your own work in order to just focus on your team. However, you must do your own work. You can only lead and take others into the field of self-awareness development as deep as you have gone yourself. So do not expect others to do work you've not done. Another's journey in this space will be unique and different so the work you have done to enable you to sit with uncertainty will serve you well in supporting others.

It is important to re-emphasize that self-awareness can only be developed if you are motivated to do so. Therefore, your team members must be both ready and motivated to do this work – just because you have done the work does not mean they need to or should want to do the work! Be very wary of forcing this onto another.

Stage one – role modelling

Sharing your own journey, including your challenges and vulnerabilities, and how it has shaped you will be of benefit. Others learn through good role models, so witnessing you doing some work in this space will be beneficial. If you work with a coach and/or therapist, let others know. If you are using a team coach, engage in the coaching process yourself. I was recently supervising a team coach who was reflecting on working on an assignment where the team leader had asked him to come and coach the team, but the team leader didn't want to be part of it – this is not role modelling behaviour. Demonstrating vulnerability and reflecting on self with your team will have a significant impact. Just be wary of making it all about you! To reflect on this, see the questions below.

> ### For Reflection
> ▶ Are you ready to support others in developing their self-awareness?
> ▶ What are you role modelling?

Stage two – create the environment

If you have worked with a coach who you trust and can open up to, you will know the power of having a psychologically safe environment. Therefore, it is imperative that you create an environment where your team feel safe, where you engage in active listening and are empathetic. This sounds easier than it is. As a leader you will come with hierarchy and a title regardless of how you show up in the space and that can project a dynamic (often unconsciously) which can be inhibiting. If there is fear of change, uncertainty around jobs or future promotions, it will be even more challenging to establish an environment to underpin facilitating the development of self-awareness.

The fundamental aspect of creating a psychologically safe environment is the creation of an environment that is based on learning and reflection, rather than diagnosis and blame. Robin and Joan Shohet's (2020) coaching supervision philosophy is helpful in underpinning how you might create this space, in that they say: 'a sandpit in which to play, rather than a courtroom in which to judge'. Amy Edmonson (2018) highlights the following top five factors to create a psychologically safe environment:

1. Ensure all team members feel valued and respected. Make sure you find time to say good morning, ask about family, say thank you and so much more.

2. Enable the asking of questions and reflections on mistakes and encourage thinking about how the team can learn from mistakes – remember no one is perfect and everyone makes mistakes.

3. Encourage and empower everyone to contribute and offer ideas, remembering to acknowledge and value those ideas even if they are not taken forward.

4. Allow for disagreement and constructive debate – there is never one way or the way, there are always more perspectives.

5. Allow for the taking of appropriate risks without any negative consequences.

Your team members must be clear on your intent and objective, so get clear on this first. You might wish to reflect on the following questions.

> **For Reflection**
>
> ▶ What is your intent in wanting others to develop their self-awareness?
>
> ▶ What is in it for you? Them? The team? The organization?
>
> ▶ What are your objectives?

Stage three – developing self-awareness in others

There are many ways you might do this, and it will probably require using a variety of approaches, as one technique might be more effective with some members than others – there is not a one size fits all approach! Neither is there a 'quick win.' I have experienced many leaders who desire a 'quick win' and short interventions, but one- or two-day leadership or team development programmes are unlikely to have sustainable long-term results as this is ongoing work.

Providing feedback

Providing feedback in a supportive way can really support the development of self-awareness. It is important to find time for positive, affirmational feedback as well as the critical and constructive feedback. I find many managers and leaders find time for the constructive feedback, but very rarely make time for the positive. Remembering self-awareness is about 'all' of who we are, and it is essential that feedback from both angles is provided. However, the old-fashioned advice of giving feedback as a sandwich (i.e. good, bad, good) is a waste of time as the individual receiving the feedback will likely only hear the negative and delete the rest. Therefore, avoid giving positive and constructive feedback on the same occasion. As Disraeli said: 'The greatest good you can do for another is not just share your riches, but to reveal to him his own.'

Giving good and meaningful feedback is a skill which requires practice. Here are a few top tips in giving impactful feedback:

- *Be succinct.* Avoid lots of 'white noise' and talking around the key message. Get clear on what is it that you most want to be heard, perhaps think about it like a newspaper headline – what's the essence of the feedback you want to deliver?

- *Be specific.* Avoid generalizations and lots of waffle. Instead, draw on specific situations/events and make it as objective as possible by providing an example.

- *Own the feedback.* Make sure you deliver the feedback from your own perspective, e.g. 'I feel'; 'I observed'; or 'I noticed'. Avoid 'it has come to my attention' or 'someone told me'. The person's mind on the receiving end will become preoccupied with 'who said that?'

- *Finish and hold the space*. Once you have delivered your feedback – *stop* talking and allow the feedback to land so that the person receiving it can process what they have heard.

- *Be empathetic and compassionate*. Deliver the message from a position of compassion, so before you deliver the feedback get clear on what your intent is in giving this feedback. Be prepared to answer clarifying questions.

- *Don't be surprised if the person receiving the feedback is defensive*. Very few people accept feedback straight away – they need time to process it and reflect, so do not expect instant acceptance. The key here is to get clear on how you will handle defensiveness, rationalization and justification so you avoid getting hooked into a 'ping-pong' match of who's right or wrong.

Provide opportunities for reflection

Think about creating the space for your team members to reflect either in a one-to-one or a team setting. Perhaps creating some form of reflective practice at the start or end of meetings or projects. Alternatively use reflective open questions. A few examples of questions you could use are:

- If a fly on the wall was observing you, what would they notice?

- If you were in the other person's shoes, how would he/she feel? How might he/she respond?

- What is it about that person/situation that is upsetting/annoying/irritating you?

- What's at stake for you?

- What's important to you about___?

- What's important to you?
- How are you feeling?
- What do you most want___?
- What do you need here?
- Which of your strengths did you draw on in this project?
- What would you do differently next time?
- What are you learning about yourself?

Use of tools and techniques

There are a variety of other tools you can use to support your team in developing self-awareness but be explicit that this is for the purpose of developing self-awareness.

Coaching

Using a coach can be of benefit. For the coaching to be of maximum value it is essential that:

The individual understands what coaching is; why he/she is receiving it; what the expectations are and what the objectives for the coaching are. It is essential that the individual is aware of your objectives and purpose in arranging the coaching.

You are clear on how you will review progress with the coachee and you know what a successful coaching intervention will be.

Agree how and when you will receive feedback. The coaching sessions themselves will be confidential. Therefore, agree how and when you will receive any feedback from the coaching. Avoid handing responsibility to the coach and stay interested by checking in with the individual as to how they are finding the coaching and what's emerging.

Also, you can increase engagement in the coaching by giving the individual some choice as to who their coach is, and it is recommended that they meet two or three coaches for an exploratory call before choosing one.

In thinking about and setting up the coaching for your team member here are some questions to think about:

- What do you want the coaching to achieve? What do you want to be different because of the coaching?
- How will you know the coaching has been successful?
- How will you review the coaching?
- What's in scope and out of scope for this coaching assignment?

Psychometric tools
As discussed in Chapter 3, there are some watchouts with using psychometric personality profiles. And it is important that you avoid making generalizations and putting people in boxes. However, these can be useful tools in starting a conversation and can provide a common language to start having discussions particularly if you do this as a team. As the leader, ensure you role-model that there is not one preferred or best profile from the results. I recall one leader who used a psychometric in his organization and he then wanted to assess others based on his – how similar were they to himself? This was because he felt this was the best – not very inclusive. If you do go down this route, use a qualified and licensed facilitator or coach who can facilitate the reflection and reviews.

360-degree review
Using a 360-degree review process with review and reflection is another approach. If you are engaged in the review, ensure

you use reflective questions, rather than giving 'you should' style feedback or questions like 'don't you think it would be a good idea if___' These sort of leading comments and questions will elicit a defensive response and are based on your ego.

> **For Reflection**
>
> Before moving to the next chapter, take a moment to reflect:
>
> You can play a valuable role in supporting the development of self-awareness in others, but only if you role-model doing the work yourself. Please remember though not all your team will want to, be ready to or believe they need to develop their self-awareness.

Further Resources

To support you in creating the environment to support others in developing self-awareness:

- Edmondson, A. C. (2018). *The fearless organization: Creating psychological safety in the workplace for learning, innovation, and growth*. Wiley. UK.

- Stone, D. & Heen, S. (2015). *Thanks for the feedback: The science and art of receiving feedback well*. Penguin.

Chapter 14
Final words

> *'This is an infinite game, where doing
> the work is the win.'*
> *Author, 2025*

Self-awareness can only come about by understanding and knowing what the construct is, and that it takes a motivated mindset of curiosity and reflection to develop it. Through the process of developing self-awareness and self-knowledge, we can start to move towards self-acceptance and then self-connection, which will enable identification of your authentic self. This is about having an unconditional acceptance of all of who you are, including your shadow side and uglies. It is in this place where you start to know, believe and embody that you are good enough, that you can let your ego settle and get out of the way and thereby enable you to connect with others on a deeper level. You will hopefully be able to answer now with confidence:

- Who are you as a leader?
- If I had your team in the room, how would they describe your leadership?

- What will your leadership legacy be?
- What's important to you?

You will have developed 'an assuredness of who you are', which will 'instil in you an unconditional acceptance of others and, because of this, the great and positive experiences of your people at work will be even greater' (Hofmann, 2020; p. 52). You will have a more cohesive team who feel valued and appreciated. You will be more comfortable to sit with uncertainty and will have developed the negative capability to lead in a VUCA world with resilience.

This is a lifetime's work which never stops, because it is 'an elusive image that slips away from us as soon as we feel we can grasp it' (Barrett, 2023; p. 37). The journey can feel exhausting and the never-ending nature of it frustrating, but that is the difference between self-awareness and self-delusion or hubris. And remember that 'doing the work' is the win, rather than the outcome of the work being the win. That is why when leaders say to me 'I am self-aware', I know they are not. It is only those who respect the philosophy that this is an ongoing journey who are really making moves towards becoming and being self-aware.

For those of you who like measurement and statistics, I have not devised, nor do I recommend a measure of self-awareness. A measure provides a static result, but this is a dynamic and fluid construct that is ever changing, and a measure is contradictory to accepting the spirit of embracing uncertainties and being okay with not knowing. There are some measures which look at levels of self-insight and self-reflection, for example, *The Self-Reflection and Self-Insight Scale* (Grant et al, 2002) but not one that measures self-awareness and gives you a score.

There is a school of thought that we can only change to the extent the system will allow. This is why two-day, off-site leadership development interventions don't always have a long-term impact. On these events, individuals commit to making a change and then return to their everyday system where nothing has changed, and they then resort back to the way they were. I remember a boss once who returned from a leadership development programme and announced that he had some new insight of how he was showing up as a leader and he was going to make some changes – nothing changed – he continued to cancel his one-to-one catch-ups with team members with no notice. With that in mind, think about what you need to change around you to support your longer-term self-acceptance – this often involves the people and activities you spend time with and doing. Of course, we can't always change those we spend time with but do notice who hampers and hinders your levels of self-connection and aim to minimize time spent with these people.

To overcome the exhaustion and frustration of the continuing nature of the work, think about undertaking this work with self-compassion and a growth mindset, recognizing that you are never the finished product and are always growing and developing. As children, if we built a sandcastle and it wasn't any good or didn't come out of the bucket properly, we just started again and built a new one, without any self-flagellation or engagement of the inner-critical voice of *'you are useless, rubbish; you are a failure etc.'*, so do this work with a child's mindset of *'I can always build another sandcastle.'* Be experimental. If you start to move from reflection to rumination, catch yourself and find some support, because rumination is destructive and anxiety inducing. Noting that this work is only effective when we do it through a lens of self-compassion means it is important to extend compassion to those we lead.

This is also my personal journey in believing 'I am good enough' so that I can operate with 'unconditional positive regard' in all aspects of my life. Whilst my research into this topic has given me knowledge, I know that there is still work to do in 'being good enough' outside of my professional life; and therefore, I don't, for one moment, believe I have reached the place of self-connection and so I continue to journey along that path. I am lucky that my client work provides me with an ongoing opportunity to 'look in the mirror' and reflect. I continue to work with a therapist, coaching supervisor and thinking partner to keep me on track when I get derailed and help me move forwards.

In this polarized world, with the advancement of technology and artificial intelligence, the leadership differentiator will ultimately come down to human connection and humanity. The route through to that human connection is self-connection. This work is needed now more than ever. Just imagine a workplace and world where there is true human connection.

For Reflection

As we come to the end of this book ask yourself:

- What do I now think about self-awareness?
- What one small step can I take today to deepen my self-connection?
- What one thing can I do to support my team on this journey?

Appendix: Other helpful resources

You can find my published papers, posts about self-awareness and reflective exercises on www.youarenotasselfawareasyouthink.com and on www.carden-consulting.co.uk

Other references, Ted Talks and Podcasts which I have found useful in developing self-awareness:

Books

Brown, B. (2015). *Rising strong*. Random House. London. UK.

Brown, B. (2021). *Atlas of the heart*. Random House. London. UK.

Kets De Vries, M.F.R. (2014). *Mindful leadership coaching: Journeys into the interior*. Macmillan Publishers Ltd. UK.

Kline, N. (2020). *The promise that changes everything: I won't interrupt you*. Penguin. London, UK.

Lama, Dalai & Tutu, D. (2016). *The book of joy*. Hutchinson. UK.

Shragai, N. (2021). *The man who mistook his job for his life.* W H Allen. UK.

Weaver, L (2017). *Rushing woman's syndrome: The impact of a never-ending to-do list and how to stay healthy in today's busy world.* Hay House Publishing. London, UK.

TED Talks

Brene Brown: www.youtube.com/watch?v=iCvmsMzlF7o

Sara Gilman and Boundaries: www.youtube.com/watch?v=rtsHUeKnkC8

Amy Edmonson & Psychological Safety: www.youtube.com/watch?v=LhoLuui9gX8

Podcasts

Author talking about self-awareness: www.associationforcoaching.com/page/dl-hub_podcast-channel-self-awareness-insight-tools-reflective-coach-development

podcasts.apple.com/gb/podcast/this-is-me-self-awareness-and-leadership-with-julia-carden/id1696614711?i=1000650547100

Dr Nia Thomas Podcast: podcasts.apple.com/gb/podcast/the-knowing-self-knowing-others-podcast/id1640336716

Steve Peters talking to the High-Performance Team: www.thehighperformancepodcast.com/podcast/steve-peters

Apps

Headspace App: www.headspace.com

Be Calm: www.calm.com/

Buddhify: www.buddhify.com/

References

Aquilina, E. (2016). *Embodying authenticity: A somatic path to transforming self, team and organisation*. Troubador Publishing Ltd. Market Harborough, UK.

Barrett, L. (2023). *A Jungian approach to coaching*. Routledge. London, UK.

Barrett, L. F., Quigley, K. S., Bliss-Moreau, E. & Aronson, K. R. (2004). Interoceptive sensitivity and self-reports of emotional experience in *Journal of Personality and Social Psychology*, 87 (5), 684.

Bion, W. R. (1962). The psycho-analytic study of thinking in *International Journal of Psychoanalysis*, 43 (4–5), 306–310.

Birch, J. (Ed.). (2021). *Coaching supervision groups: Resourcing practitioners*. Routledge. London, UK.

Blakey, J. & Day, I. (2012). *Challenging coaching: Going beyond traditional coaching to face the FACTS*. Nicholas Brealey International. London, UK.

Brown, B. (2015). *Rising strong*. Random House. London, UK.

Brown, B. (2021). *Atlas of the heart*. Random House. London, UK.

Brown, B. (2022). *The gifts of imperfection: Let go of who you think you're supposed to be and embrace who you are*. Simon and Schuster. New York City, USA.

Cameron, O. G. (2001). Interoception: The inside story – a model for psychosomatic processes in *Psychosomatic Medicine*, 63 (5), 697–710.

Carden, J., Jones, R. J. & Passmore, J. (2022a). Defining self-awareness in the context of adult development: A systematic literature review in *Journal of Management Education*, 46 (1), 140–177.

Carden, J., Passmore, J. & Jones, R. J. (2022b). Exploring the role of self-awareness in coach development: A grounded theory study in *International Journal of Training and Development*, 26 (2), 343–363.

Carse, J. (2011). *Finite and infinite games*. Simon and Schuster. New York City, USA.

Casey, L. J., Van Rooy, K. M., Sutherland, S. J., Jenkins, S. M., Rosedahl, J. K., Wood, N. G. & Clark, M. M. (2018). Improved self-acceptance, quality of life, and stress level from participation in a worksite yoga foundations program: a pilot study in *International Journal of Yoga Therapy*, 28 (1), 15–21.

Chodron, P. (2008). *The pocket Pema Chodron*. Shambhala Publications. Boulder, USA.

Collins, J. (2001). *Good to great: Why some companies make the leap and others don't*. Instaread. San Francisco, USA.

Cuddy, A. (2015). *Presence: bringing your boldest self to your biggest challenges.* Little Brown Spark. New York City, USA.

Edmondson, A. C. (2018). *The fearless organization: Creating psychological safety in the workplace for learning, innovation, and growth.* Wiley. Hoboken, USA.

Eurich, T. (2017). *Insight: Power of self-awareness in a self-deluded world.* Macmillan. London, UK.

Frankl, V. E. (1985). *Man's search for meaning.* Simon and Schuster. New York City, USA.

Fredrickson, B. (2011). *Positivity: Groundbreaking research to release your inner optimist and thrive.* One World Publications. London, UK.

Gergen, K. J. (2009). *Relational being.* Oxford University Press. Oxford, UK.

Goffee, R. & Jones, G. (2006). *Why should anyone be led by You?* Harvard Business Review Press. Boston, USA.

Goleman, D. (2021). *Leadership: The power of emotional intelligence.* More Than Sound LLC. Bothell, USA.

Grant, A. M., Franklin, J. & Langford, P. (2002). The self-reflection and insight scale: A new measure of private self-consciousness in *Social Behavior and Personality: an international journal*, 30 (8), 821–835.

Hill, S. (2023 – 2nd Edn). *Where did you learn to behave like that?* Dialogix Ltd. Cheltenham, UK.

Hofmann, Y. Y. (2020). *Beyond engagement.* Authors Place Press. Bloomington, USA.

Hollis, J. (2007). *Why good people do bad things: Understanding our darker selves.* Penguin. London, UK.

Honey, P. & Mumford, A. (1982). *The manual of learning styles.* Peter Honey Publications. Maidenhead, UK.

Kets De Vries, M. (2014). *Mindful leadership coaching. Journeys into the interior.* Palgrave Macmillan. London, UK.

Kline, N. (2009). *More time to think: A way of being in the world.* Fisher King Publishing. Thirsk, UK.

Kline, N. (2020). *The promise that changes everything: I won't interrupt you.* Penguin. London, UK.

Kolb, D. A. (1984). *Experiential learning: Experience as the source of learning and development.* Prentice-Hall. New Jersey, USA.

Luft, J. & Ingham, H. (1955). The Johari window, a graphic model of interpersonal awareness in *Proceedings of the Western Training Laboratory in Group Development.* University of California, Los Angeles. Los Angeles.

Milne, A. A. (1926). *Winnie the Pooh.* Methuen. Malton, UK.

Nestor, J. (2021). *Breath: Improve your health and wellbeing by discovering the lost art of breathing.* Penguin. London, UK.

Owen, D. (2012). *Hubris: The road to Donald Trump: Power, populism, narcissism.* Methuen. London, UK. Revised Edn 2020.

Pashler, H., McDaniel, M., Rohrer, D. & Bjork, R. (2008). Learning styles: Concepts and evidence in *Psychological science in the public interest*, 9 (3), 105–119.

Pemberton, C. (2015). *Resilience: A practical guide for coaches.* Open University Press. Maidenhead, UK.

Raval, M. D. (2024). The positive impact of mantra-based meditation: A comprehensive review in *The International Journal of Commerce and Management*, 4 (1).

Rochat, P (2018). The ontogeny of human self-consciousness in *Current Directions in Psychological Science*, 27 (5), 345–350.

Shohet, R. & Shohet, J. (2020). *In love with supervision: Creating transformative conversation*. PCCS Books. Monmouth, UK.

Shragai, N. (2021). *The man who mistook his job for his life.* W H Allen. London, UK.

Stewart, I. & Joines, V. (2012). *TA today: A new introduction to transactional analysis.* Lifespace Publishing. Chapel Hill, USA.

Stone, D. & Heen, S. (2015). *Thanks for the feedback: The science and art of receiving feedback well*. Penguin. London, UK.

van Nieuwerburgh, C. & Love, D. (2025). *Your essential guide to effective reflective practice: Improving practice through self-reflection and writing.* SAGE Publications Limited. London, UK.

Vazire, S. & Carlson, E. N. (2010). Self-knowledge of personality: Do people know themselves? in *Social and Personality Psychology Compass*, 4 (8), 605–620.

Wikipedia 16 January (2025). https://en.wikipedia.org/wiki/Somatics

Index

Page numbers in *italics* and **bold** denote figures and tables, respectively.

A
abandoned child, as childhood archetype 91
adult ego state (Berne) 140, 147, 152
affection 114–115
annoying behaviours 60–61
Aquilina, E. 134
assumptions 162–163
authentic leaders 2

B
Banzhaf, J. F. 133
behaviours 63–66
 and body language 63–64
 and facial expressions 63–64
 and mirrors 66
 noticing 67
 recording 68–69
 and systemic thinking 66
 and 360-degree feedback 69
 working with a coach 67–68
beliefs 77–79
 helpful and unhelpful 78–79
 and self-connection 142
Berne, E. 140
Bion, W. 18
black and white thinking 49
Blakey, J. 14, 68
body language 63–64
body scan technique 133
body work 132, 146–147
breathwork meditation 133
Brown, B. 3, 18, 139–140, 152

C
capacity
 to handle uncertainty 3, 5, 18
 reflecting on 33

carer child, as childhood archetype 91
CBT/CBC and thinking traps 126–127
centring practice 134–135
childhood archetypes
 abandoned child 91
 carer child 91
 compelled child 92–93
 complaint child 91
 injured child 90
 loved and respected child 93–94
 over-protect child 93
 star child 90–91
 try-harder child 92
 unfairly accused child 92
 unrecognized child 93
childhood story work 104
Chodron, P. 10
coaching 67–68, 87–88, 171–172
Collins, J. 11
comparison, and self-connection 152–153
compelled child, as childhood archetype 92–93
complaint child, as childhood archetype 91
confirmatory bias 159
conflict, and motivations 116–117
confrontation 163
controlling ability 114, 127
Cuddy, A. 64, 146

D
daily mantras 148, 153
Day, I. 14, 68
Dilts, R. 77
Disraeli, B. 169
drawing 82

E
embodied reflection 133
emotional intelligence 28
emotional literacy 125
emotions/feelings 120–121
environment, significance of 167–168
Eurich, T. 48
experiential learning 35
external self-awareness 48

F
facial expressions 63–64
feedback 169
 good and meaningful, characteristics of 169–170
 seeking 161–162
 360-degree review 59–60, 69, 172–173
feeling and thoughts, identification of 122–123, 124
filtering 49
finger pointing 69
FIRO B (psychometric test) 113–115
 affection 114–115
 control 114
 inclusion 114
fortune telling 49
Frankl, V. 120, 121, 122
free-fall writing 105–106
Freud, S. 88

G
Gergen, K. J. 140
Gestalt psychology 140
Goffee, R. 14
Goleman, D. 28
growth mindset 177

H
Hanks, T. 18
Hill, S. 90, 111
Hofmann, Y. 17
hubris 159, 176

Index

Hubris (Owen) 44
humility 18, 162

I
imposter syndrome 3
incisive questions 147
inclusion 114
individuation 17
injured child, as childhood archetype 90
internal mental state 119–120
 CBT/CBC and thinking traps 126–127
 controlling ability 127
 deepening 123
 emotional literacy 125
 emotions/feelings 120–121
 exercise starting point 121
 feeling and thoughts, identification of 122–123, 124
 journalling 125
 and pausing 122
 and self-connection 143
 self-questioning 123
 stimulus and triggers, identification of 122, 124
 thinking pairs 126
interoception *see* physiological responses
inter-personal ingredients 25, 26, 49–50, 140, 142
 behaviours *see* behaviours
 development of 50
 perception of others *see* perception of others
 and self-connection 142
 thinking traps and distortions 48–50
intra-personal ingredients 25, 26, 72–74
 internal mental state *see* internal mental state
 physiological responses *see* physiological responses
 and self-consciousness 27–28

strengths and weakness *see* strengths and weakness
values and beliefs *see* values and beliefs
irritating behaviours 60–61

J
Johari Window 5, 26, 72
Jones, G. 14
journalling 42–43
 feelings, mood and thoughts 125
 physiological responses 133
 and self-connection 148–149
 strengths and weaknesses 104–105
 values and beliefs 82
Jung, C. 17, 60, 100, 150

K
Keats, J. 18
Kets De Vries, M. 53
Kline, N. 34
Kolb, D. A. 37

L
labelling 50
learning on the edge 106–107
love and kindness meditation 142, 146, 152
loved and respected child, as childhood archetype 93–94

M
Maslow, A. 109
meditation 146
 breathwork meditation 133
 love and kindness 146
mindfulness practices 132–133, 146
mind-reading 49
mirror technique 66
motivations 11, 109–112
 conflict/high stakes 116–117
 FIRO B assessment 113–115
 and self-connection 143
 and values and beliefs 112–113

N
negative capability 3, 18, 138
negative self-talk 147
NLP training 77

O
over-protect child, as childhood archetype 93
Owen, D. 44

P
parts integration, and self-connection 149–150
pausing, and mental state 122
perception of others 53–54
 and receiving feedback 57–58
 recording reactions and responses 59
 reflection post receiving feedback 58–59
 and seeking feedback 55–56
 and 360-degree feedback 59–60
personal perception of reflection 41
personal performance reports 102
personality tests 103–104
physiological responses 129–132
 centring practice 134–135
 embodied reflection 133
 mindfulness practices 132–133
 and self-connection 143–144
 yoga and Pilates 132
Pilates 132, 146
positive psychology mindset 98
projective identification 60–61
psychometric personality profiles 9

Q
questionnaires, learning style 36–37

R
readiness to engage 11